PetSmart Charities®
COMMUNITY
TNR
Tactics and Tools

By Bryan Kortis

Vision

A lifelong, loving home for every pet.

Mission

To improve the quality of life for all pets by
creating and supporting programs that save
the lives of homeless pets and promote healthy
relationships between people and pets.

PetSmart Charities, Inc.
19601 N 27th Ave., Phoenix, AZ 85027

ISBN-13: 978-1497590168

To Kiki

"The Cat Who
Went Woof"

1993-2013

TABLE OF CONTENTS

Experience has shown it is crucial to follow correct strategies and efficiently allocate available resources in order to succeed in lowering free-roaming cat populations.

Introduction

The first guide I wrote on practicing TNR on a large scale, "Implementing a Community Trap-Neuter-Return Program," was published by The Humane Society of the United States in 2007. At that time, mostly small groups and individuals practiced TNR. Few shelters or larger animal welfare agencies were directly involved and only a handful of programs regularly handled large volumes of cats. The demonstrated potential of this method to reduce free-roaming cat populations prompted interest in expanding TNR and applying it to entire towns, cities and counties. I based the original guide on my experience running Neighborhood Cats' city-wide program in New York and what I learned from other programs.

Today, only seven years later, TNR is firmly entrenched in the mainstream of animal welfare. Hundreds of municipalities, including major cities like New York, Chicago, Las Vegas, Salt Lake City, Baltimore, San Antonio, Dallas, Albuquerque, Washington, D.C., and many more, have officially endorsed TNR as their preferred approach to managing free-roaming cats and programs are firmly in place. In growing numbers, shelters are launching their own TNR programs, hiring community cat coordinators, securing grants for large projects and partnering with local feral cat groups. Animal control agencies have gotten involved and now, at almost every animal welfare conference, you'll find a workshop on TNR.

There are many reasons for this rapid growth. A pivotal moment came when The Humane Society of the United States (HSUS) issued a position statement unequivocally supportive of TNR and, concurrently, produced and distributed new videos and books on the topic. The support of one of the largest animal welfare organizations in the United States caused local policymakers to re-think any doubts they may have had about an approach many previously considered too controversial.

Other organizations played key roles as well. Best Friends Animal Society, one of the first national groups to advocate for TNR, provided direct support to budding TNR programs. PetSmart Charities launched its free-roaming cat spay/neuter grants, greatly increasing the funding available for TNR projects. Continued advocacy by Alley Cat Allies, the group which first introduced TNR to the United States, and educational materials produced by Neighborhood Cats helped further spur growth. Just as important, on the local level, hundreds of nonprofits with their thousands of volunteers kept trapping the cats, getting them spayed or neutered and improving their communities.

Opponents to TNR did not disappear, but their arguments against the method lost weight when they were unable to offer any credible alternatives for bringing cat overpopulation under control. Shelters and public officials faced a constant flood of cats and kittens and the need to euthanize large numbers. They were no longer satisfied

with the failed approaches TNR opponents advanced, including euthanizing even more cats, admonishing pet owners to keep their cats indoors or relocating the cats to sanctuaries that everyone in the animal welfare field knew did not really exist. It is one thing to complain about the supposed decimation of wildlife by free-roaming cats or bemoan the quality of these cats' lives, but quite another to propose a workable solution to reduce their numbers.

The increased acceptance of TNR in recent years has led to a shift in the discussion from whether to do it to how to do it most effectively. The shift has opened a window of opportunity to implement TNR on a community-wide scale throughout the nation. It cannot be taken for granted this window will always remain open — positive results are needed to make the embrace of TNR permanent. TNR is not magic — it does not achieve the desired effect by just doing it with a random approach. Experience has shown it is crucial to follow correct strategies and efficiently allocate available resources in order to succeed in lowering free-roaming cat populations.

I wrote this new guide to help TNR proponents do just that. The purpose is not to detail the TNR process itself, but offer a blueprint of how to use TNR to reduce overpopulation in the whole community. Every community is different and this guide, based on the collective experience gained since the original version, presents a variety of tactics and tools that can be adapted to fit the needs of each unique situation. Wise choices and careful execution will bring about the day so many of us seek, the day when millions of cats are not suffering on our streets or dying in our shelters, but are able to live out their lives treated with the compassion and respect they deserve.

Bryan Kortis
PetSmart Charities
May 2014

New terms have evolved to describe the many cats who defy simple classification.

1.

What Kind of Cat?

Traditionally, the animal welfare field has classified cats into three categories: feral, stray or pet. "Feral" cats are unsocialized and fearful of people, making them poor candidates for adoption. A "stray" cat once lived in a home, but was lost or abandoned and forced to survive on her own. Strays can usually be quickly re-socialized and adopted, if homes are available. A "pet" cat is a companion animal with an identifiable owner and home.

As TNR programs treat more and more cats, it has become apparent that many cats cannot be neatly categorized as feral, stray or pet. Barn cats, for example, are often feral but share attributes of pets because they're essentially owned by the farmers or ranchers working the land they inhabit. In some low-income communities, it is common for people to feed and care for cats and allow them into their homes. But these same people would not claim ownership or take the cats with them when they move. Other cats that people do claim as pets may in fact spend most or all of their time outdoors, freely mixing with local ferals and strays.

New terms have evolved to describe the many cats who defy simple classification. "Free-roaming" cats spend most of their time unconfined outdoors. This term focuses on lifestyle rather than temperament or ownership, and free-roaming cats can include ferals, strays and pets. Another label with growing popularity is "community" cats. The name reflects a belief that when cats are not the property of any individual, they belong to the community, which has collective responsibility for their care. This guide uses the terms free-roaming cats and community cats interchangeably.

The new terms mirror the development of TNR. To stop reproduction, TNR programs need to spay or neuter any cat who is free-roaming, whether feral, stray, owned or some combination. It is equally important that TNR programs, in order to be most effective, have the support to accomplish this — legally, financially and otherwise — from the greater community. It should not be left only to a few dedicated volunteers to do all the work and bear all the costs.

Having a clear understanding of the purpose of a TNR program from the outset will assist in resolving difficult issues after the work gets underway.

2.

The TNR Mission

The primary goal of a community TNR program is to reduce the free-roaming cat population. Other objectives include improving public health and providing as good a level of care for the cats as reasonably possible. Another goal that has emerged in recent years is the direct lowering of euthanasia at open admission shelters through Return to Field programs, discussed in Chapter 5.

Reducing the number of cats

The first municipality in the United States to implement TNR on a community-wide scale was Newburyport, Mass., in the early 1990s. Approximately 300 cats lived along the banks of the Merrimack River, the town's central business district where restaurants, boatyards and other businesses catered to an active tourist trade. Sick, malnourished cats crying out for food and newborn litters of kittens in docked boats were unwelcome additions to the environment. Initially, the community attempted to remove the cats. Approximately 20 cats who fed out of a restaurant dumpster were trapped and taken away by animal control, but 20 more cats appeared at the same location six months later.

A coalition of local stakeholders formed to seek a better solution. The Merrimack River Feline Rescue Society and the Newburyport Chamber of Commerce were joined by local officials, veterinarians and residents. The group decided to try TNR, a very new concept in this country at that time. In the first two or three years, 200 cats were trapped — half were young or friendly enough to adopt out, resulting in an immediate drop in the free-roaming population, while the other half were returned to their territory. It took several more years to capture and alter all the remaining cats, but the effort eventually achieved a 100% sterilization rate for the cats along the river. Over the next decade, the cat population gradually died out and became extinct.

The number of cats in Newburyport was small enough that their complete elimination through TNR was possible. Completely eliminating all free-roaming cats is not a realistic goal for much larger communities, but the population can be substantially lowered. When the free-roaming population drops, benefits can accrue to the community and local animal welfare system.

While 80 to 85% of the pet cat population is spayed or neutered, sterilization rates among feral cats are dramatically lower, perhaps only in the single digits. As a result, the majority of kittens originate from ferals and other community cats.[1] Open admission shelters are flooded with their offspring during the spring and fall breeding seasons, inflating intake and euthanasia rates. Aggressive trapping policies by animal control may also contribute significantly to these inflated rates. But TNR, by ending the cats' reproduction and reducing their

---

[1] J. Levy and P. Crawford, "Humane strategies for controlling feral cat populations," Journal of the American Veterinary Medical Association 225 (2004): 1354–1360.

numbers, can break the cycle and lower both intake and euthanasia. Resources once spent on capturing or euthanizing cats can be allocated to life-saving programs, like TNR, surrender prevention or adoption. Stress on staff is greatly lowered when TNR programs can offer an alternative to the certain death of so many cats on a daily basis.

Another benefit to shelters of fewer cats can be increased adoption rates. Less crowding means the cats who are in the shelter will be healthier, face less competition for homes and have more time to find adoptive families. After Newburyport, Merrimack River Feline Rescue Society continued its TNR and other spay/neuter work throughout northeastern Massachusetts. Today, kittens must be imported into the region due to a shortage caused by these efforts.

Fewer cats will also mean fewer complaints from residents and less predation on wildlife. Cats can harm wildlife directly by hunting or indirectly by competing for a common food source. While the extent of predation is hotly debated, whatever the level actually is, it will be lower if the cat population is reduced through TNR.

Improving public health

Intact free-roaming cats engage in behaviors considered nuisances. There is the noise from female cats in heat caterwauling in the middle of the night or male cats fighting for dominance, an activity largely related to mating. There is also the noxious odor caused by unaltered males spraying to mark their territory with a combination of urine and testosterone. These behaviors end when the cats are spayed or neutered. In addition, altered cats roam much less, becoming less visible and noticeable.

In rural Sanders County, Mont., most of the 11,000 residents are concentrated in five small towns. Thompson River Animal Care Shelter (TRACS) is the only shelter in the county that handles cats. Beginning in 2010 and continuing for the next two years, TRACS performed TNR on 755 cats in the five towns. PetSmart Charities provided a grant for the project. Cat-related complaint calls to the shelter dropped from 1,032 in 2009 to 166 in 2011, an 84% decline.

Public health also gains when the cats are vaccinated against rabies as required in many jurisdictions. Cats themselves are not a reservoir species of rabies, but they often share territory with rabies-prone wildlife, including raccoons, skunks and foxes. A cat could potentially catch the fatal disease from a wild animal and then expose a person to rabies. While it is extremely rare for a person to develop a full-blown case of rabies from a cat, medical treatment for a potential rabies exposure is expensive. Multiple instances of post-exposure treatment can create a strain on public health budgets.

According to public health authorities, the protection afforded by a cat's first rabies vaccination is one year. If a second shot is given at the appropriate time, expected duration is normally three years.[2] If cats do not receive a second vaccination, protection may not extend

---

2 New Jersey Department of Health and Senior Services, "Duration of Immunity from Three or Four-Year Rabies Vaccinations," (Jan. 2012); see www.state.nj.us/health/cd/izdp/documents/duration_rabies_vaccine.pdf.

through the cats' lifetimes and the public health benefit will be less. As TNR continues to grow as a practice, caretakers should be encouraged to re-capture and update vaccinations on as many of their colony cats as possible, especially if cats are in an area where rabies is known to be present.

The cats' welfare

After being altered and released, cats may live for many years and their humane care and well-being is an important goal for its own sake. A community TNR program that deals with a large volume of cats cannot itself assume responsibility for all the cats it releases — this would be too large a financial and logistical burden. What a program can do is support the caretakers, the people who provide for the cats on a daily basis.

Caretakers are the foundation of a TNR program. They come from every profession and income level and share a sense of compassion towards the cats. Typically, they did not plan to manage a cat colony, but came upon a group of cats in need near where they live or work and responded by feeding them. While they don't view themselves as owners, the bonds they form with their free-roaming wards are as strong as those an owner feels for her pets.

A TNR program can offer caretakers training on trapping and colony care, no- or low-cost surgeries, free trap loans, shelter giveaways and food banks. Setting up an alert system for eartipped cats[3] brought to shelters will save lives and build caretaker confidence in the program. Providing mediation services for conflicts with neighbors, property managers or local officials is another form of valuable assistance. Anything that can be done to make things easier for caretakers will strengthen the overall program, get more cats sterilized faster and improve the cats' welfare.

---

[3] To identify a free-roaming cat as spayed or neutered, one ear is "tipped" during the surgery – a quarter of an inch is removed off the top of the ear in a straight line cut. Typically this is done on the left ear, although on the West Coast of the United States, the right ear is used.

There will be times when a caretaker cannot be identified. In these cases, what is in the cat's or colony's best interests and how the TNR program can help with their future care will have to be determined on a case-by-case basis. During a trapping, there may be a cat caught who has never been seen before and is likely, upon release, to run off to his unknown home. If he appears healthy and of normal weight, it is reasonable to assume he is doing well wherever he came from and he can be let go after he is neutered. Or perhaps a large colony may live in an industrial park where multiple people occasionally leave out food, but no one person has assumed full responsibility for the cats' care. After the cats are altered and returned, the TNR program could play an organizing role, setting up feeding stations and a schedule for putting out food.

It would be a mistake for a community TNR program to only focus on sterilizing cats to the exclusion of efforts to assist with their long-term well-being. Supporting caretakers will keep the program in touch with what is happening on the streets and help build a network of people who care about the cats and are willing to act on their behalf.

Using the TNR mission as a guidepost

Having a clear understanding of the purpose of a TNR program from the outset will assist in resolving difficult issues after the work gets underway. Some important questions to consider include:

Should every cat be tested for FIV and FeLV?

The primary mission of a community TNR program is to reduce the number of cats, not to prevent the spread of diseases like feline leukemia (FeLV) and feline immunodeficiency virus (FIV). Funds spent on testing are not spent on spay/neuter efforts, so the more cats tested, the fewer are sterilized, making the program less effective. This is the main reason the great majority of TNR programs do not test every cat they treat, but only those who are candidates for adoption or are ill and in need of diagnosis. In addition, research has shown the prevalence of FIV and FeLV in the free-roaming cat population is low and similar to the pet cat population.[4] The argument can be made that spay/neuter programs, by cutting off the common routes of transmission of the viruses — males fighting (FIV) and mothers nursing (FeLV) — provide more effective means of disease prevention, anyway.[5]

Should attempts be made to socialize/adopt four-month-old feral kittens?

Every TNR program faces the question of what to do about the "tweeners," the cats who are young enough to still look like kittens but old enough to be feral and difficult to socialize. There is often an impulse to hold onto these kittens in order to tame them and eventually adopt them out. The problem is this process drains resources, including funds and volunteer time that might otherwise be spent

---

[4] J. Wallace and J. Levy, "Population characteristics of feral cats admitted to seven trap-neuter-return programs in the United States," Journal of Feline Medicine and Surgery 8 (2006): 279–284. Irene Lee and Julie K. Levy, "Prevalence of feline leukemia virus infection and serum antibodies against feline immunodeficiency virus in unowned free-roaming cats," Journal of the American Veterinary Medical Association 220 (2002): 620-622.

[5] For more on the issue of testing, see "Neighborhood Cats TNR Handbook," 2nd ed. (2013), Chapter 13, p. 120; free download at www.neighborhoodcats.org.

trapping and altering more cats. Lowering the number of free-roaming cats is going to be accomplished faster if TNR programs do not take on this task.

Should cats be relocated when people don't want them back?

There will be residents who are fine with the cats being trapped and sterilized, but who will want them relocated instead of returned. They may be afraid of neighbors who are angry at the cats and may have threatened them. Or they may simply not want the cats around anymore.

Performing a successful relocation can be time-consuming, uncertain and expensive. First, a suitable new site with a committed caretaker must be located. Then the cats must be trapped, provided veterinary treatment which may include spaying and neutering, transported and kept confined at the new location for up to three weeks. Even if everything is done correctly, there is no guarantee all the cats will stick around upon release. In addition, food and shelter must be permanently removed from the cats' original territory to prevent new cats from moving in and starting a new colony.

Because the required resources can be a drain on a TNR program, relocations should only be performed in extreme circumstances, such as major demolition at a colony site, closing of a factory or the passing away of a caretaker with no one in the area willing to take over the feeding. Otherwise, politely but firmly inform people the cats are coming back. This approach is rarely a problem in the long run. When people are angry about the cats or don't want them around, it is usually because of the cats' nuisance behavior. Spay/neuter surgeries resolve these behaviors, causing most complaints and animosity to dissipate.

The bottom line is that every community TNR program is going to face a limit on how much it can accomplish. All problems involving cats cannot be addressed. Keeping the primary mission foremost in mind — to reduce the number of community cats — will help guide the best use of resources and maximize the program's impact.

Discovering how best to knit these tactics together and adapt them to local needs is the cutting edge of TNR today.

3.

Tactics: An Overview

The three major tactics a community TNR program can employ are (1) targeting, (2) Return to Field and (3) grassroots mobilization (Figure 1). Subsequent chapters will explore each tactic in detail. This section provides a brief overview.

Figure 1.
Three tactics of a community TNR program

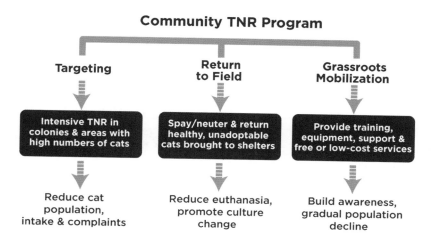

Community TNR Program

Targeting	Return to Field	Grassroots Mobilization
Intensive TNR in colonies & areas with high numbers of cats	Spay/neuter & return healthy, unadoptable cats brought to shelters	Provide training, equipment, support & free or low-cost services
Reduce cat population, intake & complaints	Reduce euthanasia, promote culture change	Build awareness, gradual population decline

Targeting refers to getting most or all of the cats in a given area spayed or neutered. It is the opposite of doing TNR randomly and altering cats on more or less of a first-come, first-served basis without regard to where they originate. Targeting can be performed on both a colony and community level. When targeting a colony, the goal is to sterilize all the cats in that specific group. Achieving a 100% sterilization rate will eliminate reproduction, creating the best opportunity for the cats' numbers to decline over time. On the community level, targeting involves concentrating resources, like surgeries, personnel and marketing, in part of the community — such as a neighborhood or ZIP code — in order to TNR a substantial percentage of the free-roaming cats in that section. Targeting parts of the community and not only colonies increases the pace of population reduction.

Return to Field is a shelter-based program focusing on free-roaming cats who are brought to a shelter. Such cats would normally be euthanized either because they are feral or there is no room to hold them. Return to Field offers an alternative: sterilizing these cats and releasing them back to their locations of origin. Euthanasia rates drop, sometimes dramatically, and the local culture, both inside and outside the shelter, may be transformed in a positive way.

The goal of grassroots mobilization is to have caretakers and the public provide the workforce and resources for TNR'ing colonies throughout the community. To accomplish this, a TNR program can offer training, equipment, discount surgeries, coaching and other services. These build awareness and support for TNR programs and help achieve gradual population reduction.

All three tactics are relatively new. Grassroots mobilization emerged in the early 2000s when a few TNR programs, most notably Neighborhood Cats in New York City, started training and recruiting community members on a large scale. The first known Return to Field program was launched in 2008 in Jacksonville,

Fla., by Jacksonville Animal Care & Protective Services, First Coast No More Homeless Pets and Best Friends Animal Society. The practice of targeting has grown rapidly since the fall of 2009 when PetSmart Charities, the nation's largest TNR funder, made targeting a requirement for its free-roaming cat spay/neuter grants.

The tactics are not exclusive and can be combined. Training and equipping caretakers to target colonies should be part of any grassroots mobilization effort. A Return to Field program that incorporates targeting on either a colony or community level can impact not only euthanasia, but reduce the community cat population as well. While caretakers throughout a community are assisted in altering their individual colonies, TNR program staff and volunteers can target narrow sections with disproportionately large cat populations. Discovering how best to knit these tactics together and adapt them to local needs is the cutting edge of TNR today.

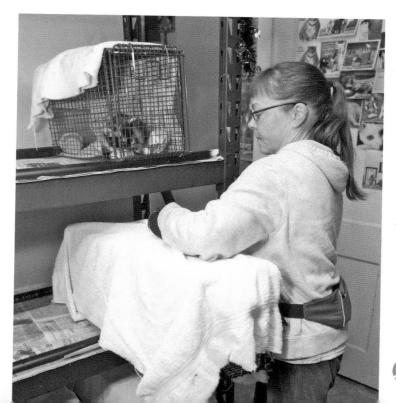

Making good tactical choices in allocating surgeries and other TNR resources is critical to success. When no targeting is done, there is no population decline.

4.
Targeting

When the idea of starting a community TNR program is first considered, the problem to be addressed may feel overwhelming. Estimates of the number of free-roaming cats may run into the hundreds, thousands or more. Facing these numbers, available resources may seem too few and inadequate for the scale of need. But progress can be made nonetheless if these resources are allocated efficiently to achieve the maximum benefit in terms of population reduction. That is what targeting is all about.

Colony-level targeting

The "colony" is the basic unit of TNR. It refers to a group of free-roaming cats who share a common food source and live in the same territory. While there may be some migration between colonies in the same area, for the most part they are distinct units and can range in size from even one cat to hundreds. To understand how targeting can reduce numbers, it is helpful to first examine a single colony of community cats.

Figure 2 depicts a colony of 10 cats living in the backyards of one neighborhood.

If two of the cats are spayed or neutered, the sterilization rate for the colony will be 20% (Figure 3). A rate this low will have no impact on the size of the colony because the eight remaining unaltered cats can reproduce fast and often enough to compensate for the loss of reproductive capacity in the two sterilized cats.

If instead all 10 cats in the colony are spayed or neutered (Figure 4), reproductive capacity is eliminated and the colony is more likely to decline over time.

Several years ago, some TNR advocates believed in a popular theory known as the "70% rule," which was loosely based on mathematical principles. According to the rule, when 70% of a colony's members are sterilized, attrition equals births and colony size is stabilized. Above 70%, attrition outpaces births and the cats' numbers decrease. But there is no empirical data to support a precise sterilization percentage within a colony to achieve population reduction and the rule has been largely debunked.

While there may not be an exact, universal threshold required to achieve population decline, experience does point to the need for a high level of sterilization in order for attrition to outpace feline reproduction. If TNR in a 10-cat colony proceeds only intermittently at one or two cats at a time, the overall number of cats may not decline and the only ceiling on colony size will be the environment's carrying capacity — the amount of food and shelter available. To achieve population reduction, the goal should be to alter all the cats quickly and get as close as possible to a 100% sterilization rate.

Figure 2. 10-cat backyard colony

Figure 3. 2 of 10 cats sterilized

Figure 4. 100% sterilization

Because colonies are the basic units of TNR, colony-level targeting is essential to any strategy a community TNR program decides to pursue. When targeting a part of town responsible for high cat intake, TNR in that area should proceed colony by colony with the aim of altering all the cats in each unit. If employing grassroots mobilization, the goal is similar. If a member of the public TNR's a colony, all the cats in that colony should be sterilized.

The need to alter entire colonies also dictates how spay/neuter surgical slots should be allocated. A common practice for some TNR programs is to allocate by caretaker. If there are 100 slots available for one month and 25 caretakers who want them, the program will give each caretaker four slots. This may be fair in one sense, but it is ineffective population control. Many of the colonies those cats come from will have far more than four members. Sterilization levels may not become high enough for the number of cats in any of these colonies to gradually decrease. It would be more effective to allocate the slots by colony. For example, those 100 slots could go to 10 colonies with 10 cats in each.

For a grassroots approach, colony-level targeting requires training residents how to TNR all of their colony cats at once, beginning with "mass trapping." The instructional video, "How to Perform a Mass Trapping," can be viewed at no cost at www.neighborhoodcats.org. The process is also described in the "Neighborhood Cats TNR Handbook," available for free download at the same link.

To support mass trapping, a TNR program should make a sufficient amount of traps and other equipment available for borrowing, as it is unlikely a caretaker will buy as many traps as there are colony cats for one-time use. There must also be enough surgical capacity made available to accommodate entire colonies, allowing all the cats to be trapped and sterilized together.

Community-level targeting

When targeting is performed on the community as well as colony level, the pace of population reduction can be increased. This can be illustrated by a hypothetical community, "Feralville," with a population of 100 free-roaming cats. The cats are spread out evenly. Each of the town's four ZIP codes has 25 cats found in colonies of various sizes (Figure 5).

Assume there are only 20 surgeries available to Feralville's TNR program. That may be all the program can afford or the maximum amount of surgeries local clinics can make available.

This would be a typical situation for most communities where the number of free-roaming cats exceeds the resources needed to sterilize them all at once.

Figure 5. **100 community cats**

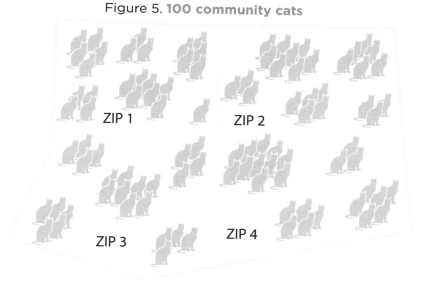

If the Feralville program sterilized 20 cats on a "first come, first served" basis, without any targeting on the colony level or otherwise, the results might appear as depicted in Figure 6, with altered cats shown in blue.

Because none of the colonies have even a majority of their cats sterilized, none will start decreasing in size because of the TNR intervention. As a result, Feralville's free-roaming cat population as a whole will not decline either. If colony-level targeting had been used, the 20 surgeries might be distributed as shown in Figure 7.

There are now five colonies with all or close to all of their members spayed or neutered. The potential exists for these colonies to start dropping in size and, to the extent they do, Feralville's community cat population will decrease. If grassroots mobilization was the sole tactic used by the Feralville program, with residents mass trapping random colonies throughout the town, the results might appear as in Figure 7.

The limitation of this grassroots approach is that each of the treated colonies remains in close proximity to other, unaltered colonies. This leaves the possibility intact cats from those nearby, untreated colonies may at some point migrate into treated colonies, start reproducing and reverse some or all of the gains made in reducing colony size.

Migration could occur for a few reasons. The populations of the intact colonies could grow beyond what their available food and shelter will support, creating pressure for cats in these colonies to leave and find more fruitful territory. It is also possible that as numbers decrease in the TNR'd colonies, there will be more food and shelter available than colony cats to take advantage of the resources. In biological terms, this will create a vacuum, encouraging cats from the intact colonies to move in and fill the vacuum. Finally, some cats are prone to explore and intact cats may come visit then decide to stay in their spayed and neutered neighbors' territory.

Figure 6. **No targeting**

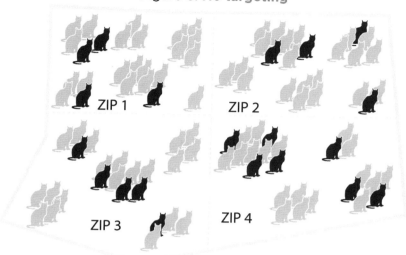

Figure 7. **Colony-level targeting**

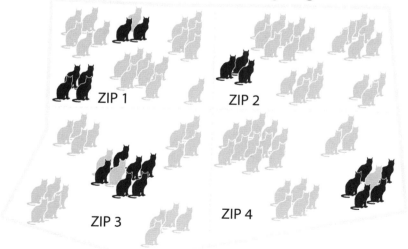

To minimize the impact of migration between colonies, the Feralville TNR program can decide, in addition to targeting colonies, to also use community-level targeting when allocating its 20 surgeries. By targeting ZIP code 4, 20 of the 25 cats in the area (80%) are altered. In addition, all four colonies in ZIP code 4 have most or all of their members sterilized (Figure 8).

Figure 8. **Community-level targeting**

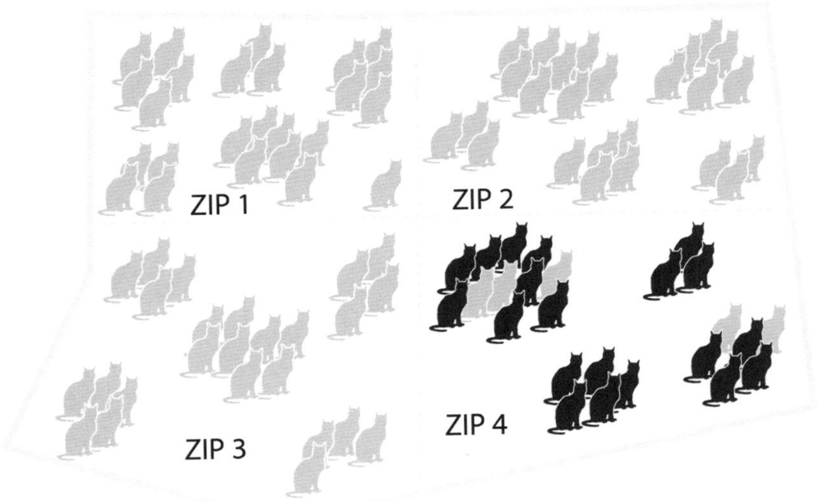

Such a high sterilization rate, plus the absence of untreated colonies, greatly reduces the possibility of migration of intact cats into TNR'd colonies within ZIP code 4. There may be some migration from colonies just across the borders, but likely not enough to reverse the downward population trend. Cats farther away in ZIP codes 1 through 3 will not travel the distance necessary to repopulate ZIP code 4.

The Feralville example reflects an overall sterilization rate of 80% with all colonies in the target area treated, but there are no precise thresholds. The goal is to get as many of the cats in a target area spayed or neutered as possible. The more cats and colonies that are altered, the more reproductive capacity and migration will be diminished and the faster the population will decline. The goal should be to alter a substantial percentage of the free-roaming cats present in the target area, proceeding colony by colony and achieving as close as possible to 100% sterilization in any colonies selected for TNR.

In sum, making good tactical choices in allocating surgeries and other TNR resources is critical to success. When no targeting is done, there is no population decline. With colony-level targeting alone, there is the potential for reduced numbers within treated colonies, but migration from surrounding intact colonies could reverse some of the drop and slow progress in reducing the community's free-roaming cat population. When using community-level targeting in addition to colony-level, migration is no longer as strong a factor, maximizing the pace and extent of population reduction.

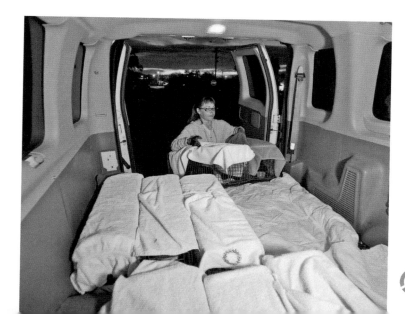

Choosing a target area

The Feralville example assumes the cats were evenly distributed throughout the town. In most communities, that is not the reality. There are almost always some areas where there are more free-roaming cats than others. Often there will be one section that has a particularly high concentration. A more typical depiction of free-roaming cat demographics is illustrated by Figure 9, which shows 50 of Feralville's 100 free-roaming cats residing in ZIP code 3, while the other 50 are spread among the remaining three ZIP codes. Targeting ZIP code 3, Feralville's "hot spot," would have the greatest impact on reducing free-roaming cat overpopulation in the community.

Figure 9 **Unequal distribution of community cats**

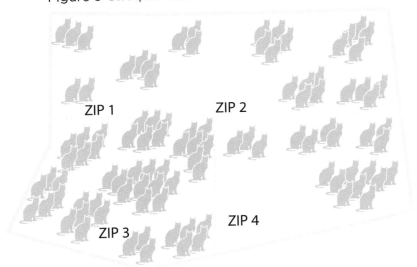

Areas with relatively high numbers of cats can be identified by examining the following:

Intake broken down by location of origin

Intake processes at most shelters include recording the location where the cat originated. Some will enter a complete address, others only the ZIP code. If the shelter is open admission — meaning no cats are turned away — intake patterns can provide a snapshot of the distribution of cats in the community. The higher the intakes from a certain area, the more cats, including free-roaming cats, are likely to be located there. One caveat: Be careful if the highest intake ZIP code is also the one in which the shelter itself is located. A common practice with data entry in shelters is to default to the shelter's ZIP code when the actual ZIP code of origin is unknown. Entering data correctly would avoid this confusion.

Also, do not rely too heavily on distinctions between "owner-surrender" cats and "strays." Theoretically, larger free-roaming cat populations could be located based on where the most cats classified as "stray" originate. But many factors can distort which category a shelter assigns to a cat. A pet owner may be embarrassed to admit she is surrendering her cat and claim he is a stray. If the shelter charges a surrender fee for owned cats and not for strays, this too could cause pet owners to say their cats are strays in order to avoid payment. A litter of kittens born outside to an unaltered pet might be reasonably classified as either stray or owner-surrender. Unless the shelter's policies and practices are designed to eliminate these distortions, a better and more objective data point is simply "cats." Age, if it is tracked correctly, can also be helpful. Most kittens are born to free-roaming cats,[6] so where large numbers of kittens originate, there are likely to be correspondingly large numbers of community cats.

---

[6] J. Levy and P. Crawford, "Humane strategies for controlling feral cat populations," Journal of the American Veterinary Medical Association Vol. 225 (2004): 1354–1360.

Complaint calls or requests for assistance

Intact free-roaming cats tend to generate a high volume of complaint calls to animal control and other municipal agencies, as well as requests for help to shelters and rescue groups. Tracking the location of the cats when someone calls to complain or ask for assistance will reveal patterns much the same way intake does. Where the most calls originate from is likely where there are the most cats.

Economic conditions

Poverty is directly correlated to unaltered cats in households.[7] Many pet owners in low-income areas cannot afford the surgery, or may lack access to conveniently located veterinary services. There could be educational issues as well regarding the value of spay/neuter surgery. Upon sexual maturity, many of these unaltered pet cats in low-income areas are placed on the streets in response to their behavioral issues, giving rise to relatively large free-roaming cat populations. Low-income areas also often have higher percentages of rental housing and transient residents are more prone to leave their unaltered cats behind when they move. This is a commonly reported scenario, for example, in mobile home parks.

Tribal knowledge

Much can be learned from the collective experience of people who have been working with animals in a specific community for a length of time. These could include rescuers, trappers, animal control officers, public health officials, humane law officers and shelter staff. While these people may not be able to point to specific data, they nonetheless know the problem areas in their community and the locations where the most cats will be found.

---

[7] K. Chu, "Population characteristics and neuter status of cats living in households in the United States," Journal of the American Veterinary Medical Association 234 (2007): 1023–1030.

Mapping tools

It can be revealing to map addresses where cats taken in to the shelter originated or where cats who people call about are located. The visual patterns are often striking, and highlight where targeting can have the most impact. These mapping tools can be found and used online or purchased as software for installation on a computer. They automatically convert information from a spreadsheet of addresses into a visual map.

Estimating the number of free-roaming cats

Before a program can sterilize a substantial percentage of the community cats in a target area, it needs to have some idea of how many cats are actually there. In most instances, it will be impractical to do an actual census and count feline noses. There are ways to realistically estimate numbers to end up in the ballpark instead of miles away. But it is important to understand the methods currently available for arriving at such numbers are just as much art as science. There is no one definitive formula to produce an exact community cat count.

Human population-based estimates

When PetSmart Charities began requiring targeting for its TNR grants in 2009, it instructed applicants to estimate the free-roaming cat population in a given area by dividing the human population by six. This was based on the recommendations of academic researchers who had performed demographic studies of community cats. However, PetSmart Charities soon realized the results were consistently and often grossly overestimating free-roaming cat populations. Grantees consistently began to see impact, such as lower intake, and began to have difficulty finding more cats in the target area after performing far fewer surgeries than the "divide by six" formula had predicted.

Taking a closer look at the academic research, PetSmart Charities found what might be methodological errors. The studies counted the number of cats fed in a defined area, then compared the result to the number of residents in that same area.[8] So, hypothetically, if 500 cats were being fed in a neighborhood with 3,000 residents, the formula arrived at would be "divide the human population by six." The possible mistake, in PetSmart Charities' view, was that the studies separately counted every cat fed, whether fed daily by one caretaker, intermittently or only once in the past year. This created the potential for a lot of double counting — the same cat could be fed daily by one household, intermittently by another and once a year by a third. But the method used would conclude there were three cats, not one. Using the same raw data, when the count is limited to only cats fed daily by the same caretaker, the formula arrived at is "divide the human population by 15."

> It is important to understand the methods currently available for arriving at such numbers are just as much art as science. There is no one definitive formula to produce an exact community cat count.

Using "divide by 15" as a starting point resulted in fewer grant projects running out of cats in their original target areas before reaching surgery goals. On a national scale, the formula gives an estimate of about 20 million community cats in the United States, which is on the low end of popular national estimates, but within the range.

Human population density and climate factors

It must be emphasized that "divide by 15" is a starting point, not an end point. The size of free-roaming cat populations varies widely according to local conditions. On one extreme, in dense urban areas where most or all people live in multi-story structures, there is a limited

8 See, and studies cited therein, Julie K. Levy, "Number of unowned free-roaming cats in a college community in the southern United States and characteristics of community residents who feed them," Journal of the American Veterinary Medical Association 223 (2003): 202-205.

amount of ground space and hence less food and shelter for feral and stray cats. As a consequence, there will be fewer cats per capita than the average location and the result of the "divide by 15" calculation will need to be revised downward to get a more accurate reading. In contrast, rural areas made up mostly of farmland have fewer people per square mile but much more space and potentially many food sources for free-roaming cats. One farmer with a barn may have 30 cats. In these situations, "divide by 15" will underestimate and the result would need to be revised upward.

Weather, too, is a factor that has to be taken into account. While feral cats have been known to survive in almost any climate, the harsh winters of the North take more of a toll than the long, warm seasons of the South. A location in a warmer climate will thus tend to have a higher number of free-roaming cats per capita than a similar setting in the colder North.

Tribal knowledge comes into play when accounting for human population density and climate because there are no standard formulas as yet for these revisions. The final estimate has to make sense to those experienced in working with free-roaming cats in that community and should be further adjusted if it does not. As the TNR work in the target area gets underway, project leaders will need to be open to the possibility that their original estimates were too high or too low and be willing to make adjustments to the overall strategy as needed.

Aligning resources with the target area

After identifying the part of the community with the highest concentration of free-roaming cats and estimating their numbers, TNR program leaders need to assess available resources. The key question is: Will the resources support altering a substantial percentage of the cats so that enough of them are sterilized to tip the balance in favor of future declines in population?

In Feralville, after ZIP code 3 is identified as the hot spot and estimated to have 50 cats, the local TNR program may find it only has 10 surgeries available. If it proceeds with the project, only two colonies will be targeted and 20% of the cats in ZIP code 3 sterilized (Figure 10). There may be some progress from two of the colonies being all or almost all spayed or neutered.

But because there are still 40 unaltered cats, it is unlikely there will be a significant impact on reducing the ZIP code 3 cat population or on intake or complaint calls. Rather than giving up on the project, the TNR program can decide to target an area where its resources match the need, such as ZIP code 1, where 10 surgeries would result in all the colonies being treated and 10 of 12 cats sterilized (Figure 11). This approach effectively uses both colony- and community-level targeting and results in the greatest amount of population reduction possible from the 10 available surgeries.

Another example might be that the Feralville program estimates there are 50 cats in ZIP code 3 and finds it has 70 surgeries available. With that many resources, the program could make the strategically sound decision

Figure 10. **Too few surgeries for target area**

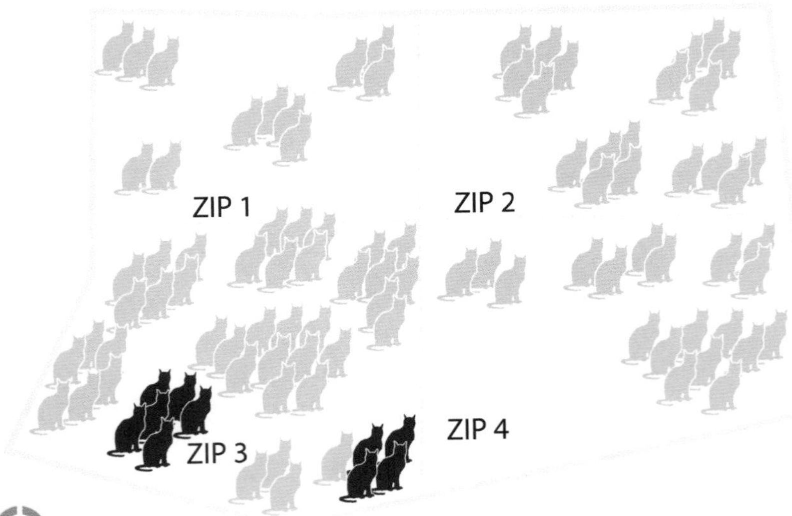

to make the entire town its target area, rather than focus on ZIP codes, and aim for an overall 70% sterilization rate (Figure 12).

Figure 11. Matching target area to available surgeries

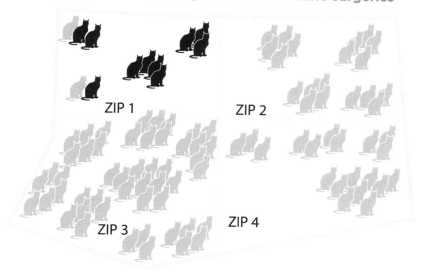

Figure 12. Targeting the entire community

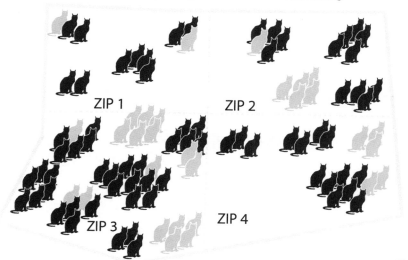

Outreach: finding cats, building trust

Making smart tactical choices is essential for the success of a TNR program, but it is not enough by itself. In the end, identifying the right target area, accurately estimating the number of cats and lining up the required resources will have little impact if the cats themselves cannot be located and trapped. Effective outreach is critical.

If TNR activity is taking place throughout a shelter or clinic's service area, available surgical slots for free-roaming cats can usually be filled by simply announcing the availability of free or heavily discounted surgeries through traditional or social media. Because the program is recruiting from the service area's entire population, it is likely enough people will hear the message and be motivated to take advantage of the opportunity.

In a much smaller target area, where fewer people reside and work, the same kind of outreach is unlikely to yield similar results. Many people caring for community cats may not hear the message, and among those who do, many may be unwilling to identify themselves and participate due to lack of trust, understanding or interest. For a targeted project to succeed, every effort must be made to reach these caretakers and persuade them to engage in the process in some manner, even if it is simply to report the cats' locations and allow trapping to

proceed. Otherwise, it may be impossible to attain the goal of altering a substantial percentage of the cats in the target area.

Traditional media, such as newspaper advertising, website posts, radio spots, newsletters, and social media such as Facebook can be used at the outset of a targeted TNR project and will likely recruit a certain number of caretakers and cats. A second wave of more targeted marketing could include postcards mailed to target-area residents or, at a lower cost, inserts in utility or tax bills sent out by the municipality. Outdoor advertising such as yard signs, a billboard or similar signage placed at a highly trafficked location in the target area may also prove fruitful. If a vehicle will be used frequently as part of the TNR work, wrapping it in attention-getting graphics or advertising could draw a lot of attention to the project.

These kinds of marketing are what might be termed "passive" — the message is put out and the TNR program waits for people to respond. When passive marketing no longer pulls in enough participants, the program will need to turn to active marketing methods to increase engagement with the target community. The best way forward will be "boots on the ground" efforts — passing out flyers and placing door hangers, attending community events and meetings, walking

the neighborhood and talking to people about the cats. These face-to-face, door-to-door actions are the most direct way to connect with the community.

The Humane Society of the United States, with support from PetSmart Charities, has pioneered spay/neuter outreach to low-income communities with a program called "Pets for Life." The program relies entirely on in-field outreach and includes offering free vaccine or wellness clinics. By being present, non-judgmental and helpful, staff build trust and educate residents on the value of spay/neuter surgeries. The initial goal is to reach pet owners, but the program has found community cat caretakers soon come forward or are identified by other residents and can be brought into the spay/neuter fold as well. The entire Pets for Life Community Outreach Toolkit can be downloaded at no cost and is highly recommended for anyone doing spay/neuter outreach, including TNR (go to www.animalsheltering.org/how-we-help/work-for-change/pets-for-life/pets-for-life-toolkit.html).

One group working on a targeted TNR project in a low-income community, Spay Worcester, a task force of the Massachusetts Animal Coalition, found a pattern in how residents related to cats. People would adopt kittens who they found on the streets and bring them into their homes (or, as the residents would say, they'd adopt kittens who "found them.") When the cats reached sexual maturity and began engaging in typical nuisance behaviors, such as vocalizing and spraying, their owners would place them back outside to live but continue to feed them, still considering the cats their pets. It was not lack of caring which caused these evictions, but either lack of education about spay/neuter benefits or, more often, lack of financial means to pay for the surgery. Understanding and respecting the strong bond between residents and their now free-roaming pets — cats who sometimes had multiple people claiming them as their own — facilitated communication and allowed Spay Worcester staff and volunteers to better intervene.

Some kinds of marketing will work in some communities and not in others, so there may be a period of trial and error at the beginning of outreach. Messaging should be tailored to the local culture whenever possible. In a heavily Hispanic community, for example, written materials should have both English and Spanish translations. Rural areas can present their own unique challenges and may require a longer than usual period of building relationships and becoming known and trusted in the community before people will participate. An informative look at how one group overcame obstacles in a rural setting can be found in the article, "The Challenge of a Rural TNR Project," by Nancy Peterson in the November-December 2013 issue of Animal Sheltering magazine (www.animalsheltering. org/resources/magazine/nov-dec-2013/).

How the agency performing the TNR project has handled free-roaming cats in the target community in the past can also impact the effectiveness of outreach. If the agency, when performing animal control functions, had previously trapped and euthanized cats, caretakers may be wary of the agency's intentions and slower to respond to outreach efforts even if policy has officially shifted to TNR. Understanding this and taking extra steps to reassure caretakers will help. Effective methods can include meetings with neighborhood associations, one-on-one talks, official pronouncements in favor of TNR and working with an animal welfare partner who is already trusted. More than anything, once people start to see cats being altered and returned, residents will be more willing to come forward and help get their colonies spayed and neutered, too.

Consider setting up a separate telephone contact number and voicemail for a TNR project. That way it will be easy for caretakers to get and offer information and not get lost in the shuffle. Many caretakers may not have Internet access so offering an alternative to an email address may expand a program's reach. Keep the outgoing telephone message short and simple — key information needed from callers will be the locations of the cats and the caretaker's contact information. Wait until directly contacting the caretaker before gathering any additional information.

While the focus of outreach will be on the target area, messaging is likely to travel beyond its borders and reach other caretakers interested in accessing the same services. Due to grant guidelines or resource restrictions, a program may not be able to offer the same level of services to caretakers outside the target area. People who don't understand this strategy may complain it isn't fair. Anticipate this and have another track of services available to offer, even if it is not as comprehensive as what is provided in the target zone. This is where employing grassroots mobilization can come in handy (see Chapter 6). While a program may not be able to have staff go trap and transport the cats and pay all the costs, it could offer training, free rental equipment and referrals for discounted spay/neuter services. This gives people an option and will improve public relations much more than saying "we can't help you."

Who does the field work?

In the field, TNR involves trapping, transporting cats and caring for them while they are confined. Many TNR programs today rely heavily on caretakers to catch and care for their cats while the programs provide services like equipment rentals and discount spay/neuter surgeries. This system can work if an entire community with a large population is being served. In that case, there will typically be enough motivated caretakers located throughout the community who will do the field work and fill available surgical slots.

The system usually does not work when a targeted TNR project is attempted in an area with a much smaller population base. If the program is targeting only a section of a large community, or an entire small community, there may not be a sufficient number of target-area caretakers willing to do the work. The reality is that many caretakers, although they genuinely care about the cats they're feeding, will not perform TNR themselves even if given the opportunity to do so at little or no cost. The process may be too physically demanding, especially for anyone elderly or disabled, the time required may be more than a caretaker is willing or able to commit, or the whole process may be too intimidating or otherwise emotionally difficult. Whatever the reasons, good or bad, many caretakers will not participate.

To be successful and achieve long-term population decline, a targeted TNR project must sterilize most of the free-roaming cats in the selected area. If the only cats sterilized are those belonging to caretakers willing to do the work themselves, there's a good chance not enough cats will be altered to make an overall difference. That was repeatedly the experience at PetSmart Charities when targeted TNR grant projects relied solely on caretakers to do the field work. With rare exception, PetSmart Charities no longer considers this an adequate plan.

To maximize effectiveness when targeting, a TNR program must have its own personnel and be prepared to perform the bulk of the trapping, transport and other work on its own. Caretaker cooperation is still required to gain information about the cats' locations and habits, provide access to private property and withhold food at the appropriate time. Any caretaker assistance beyond that will help move the project forward, but should not be an essential part of the plan.

Which personnel are assigned to the project will depend on available resources. They could be the TNR program's paid staff or own volunteers. Or the program could partner with a local TNR or rescue group, or individual trappers known to be active in the community. Personnel need to be selected carefully with the demands of the project foremost in mind. Trapping multiple cats in a colony may proceed over two or three days. Adding the time required for surgery and a day or two of recovery makes the entire process last four to six days in a row. Each day the cats are confined, they need to be fed and their traps (which serve as cages) must be cleaned twice daily. They also have to be dropped off and picked up from the spay/neuter clinic at agreed-upon times.[9]

---

[9] "The Neighborhood Cats TNR Handbook," 2nd ed., offers detailed instructions on mass trapping, and the video, "How to Perform a Mass Trapping," can also be accessed on their website at www.neighborhoodcats.org.

Depending on the total number of cats to be spayed or neutered and the time frame, the work could amount to a part-time or even full-time job. If 1,000 cats are to be captured and altered within a year, that requires a pace of about 20 cats a week. The field work process is time-consuming and requires consistent effort and attention. If assigning anyone other than paid staff, candidates should be volunteers or groups with a history of being reliable and able to maintain a sustained effort. Problems are likely to result if the program uses only individual volunteers or small, grassroots groups who can only devote limited amounts of time at inconsistent intervals.

If unsure how much a partner can do, plan on starting off small. A reasonable goal would be to aim for a couple of hundred cats over a year in a target area where it is estimated there are a few hundred. That way, the pace will not be too demanding, the program will have an opportunity to assess the strength of field personnel and, if necessary, others from the agency can step in and take over the task.

Surgeries, holding space, transportation and traps

The basic resources needed for any TNR project will also be required when targeting. Low-cost surgeries make it possible for the TNR program to treat large numbers of cats. The TNR program should plan from the outset to cover all of the costs in a targeted project and consider any contributions extra funds. While requesting donations from assisted caretakers may be a smart way to raise some money, requiring co-pays for the surgeries is not a good strategy. Again, when targeting, no cat can be left behind and mandatory co-pays will mean some cats don't get altered because the caretaker can't afford the fees or simply won't pay.

After being caught and while recovering for a day or two from surgery, the cats need to be confined. For targeted TNR programs, there should be a designated holding space accessible to field personnel for the length of the project. It could be a garage, a trailer in the shelter parking lot, a side room — anywhere that is warm, dry and secure. What should be avoided is relying on caretakers to provide holding space for each of their colonies because many caretakers will be unable to do so.

Transportation will be a constant need as well. Trapped cats will need transport to the holding space, back and forth from the spay/neuter clinic and back to their original territories. A program must also have enough equipment, including traps and trap dividers, to handle the anticipated volume of cats. It is recommended traps be of sufficient length to double as cages — either 30 or 36 inches — and have a sliding rear door to allow for feeding and cleaning both ends of the trap. Trap dividers must be sturdy enough to make it safe to open one of the trap doors while the cat is sectioned off on the opposite end.[10]

Measuring impact

Measuring the impact of the project serves two important purposes. First, it lets programs and planners know whether efforts were successful in lowering the cat population and justified the investment of resources. Metrics can also be a very helpful guide during the project itself. With targeted projects, there often comes a point when it is difficult to locate more cats. There are a couple of possible reasons why this problem occurs. There may still be plenty of cats in the targeted area, but outreach strategy is no longer working. If so, a change in outreach methods and further searching in the target area are needed. The other possibility is that the original estimate of the number of cats was

---

[10] For instructions on caring for cats held in traps, see the "Neighborhood Cats TNR Handbook," 2nd ed., Chapter 11, available for free download at www.neighborhoodcats.org. A short video of the feeding and cleaning process can be viewed on the Neighborhood Cats website.

too high and the program can't find more cats because it has already sterilized most or close to all of them. If that is the case, it is time to expand the target area and begin working somewhere new, rather than wasting time and resources trying to locate cats who aren't there.

One way to help determine which it is — there are many more cats yet to be located or there are few cats left to be found — is by evaluating impact metrics. If the target area was selected based on intake at the local open admission shelter, what do those numbers look like now midway through the project? If there is significant improvement with fewer cats coming in, that would suggest the project has altered a substantial percentage of the free-roaming population in the target area and should add new territory. If instead intake is unchanged or rising, that would suggest there are still plenty of unaltered cats needing to be caught.

The kind of metrics to use depends largely on what data is available. The most direct metric is the actual number of cats, but this can be impossible to determine in projects involving large numbers of cats over a sizeable area. It may be possible in smaller target areas, such as a mobile home park, landfill or neighborhood. Where a census of the cats is impractical, indirect metrics that reflect changes in the free-roaming population must be relied upon instead. Intake into an open admission shelter is an indirect data point — as the cat population drops, intake typically goes down, too. However, the relationship is not absolute and changes in intake can reflect other variables besides the size of the cat population, such as changes in shelter policy. For example, if animal control officers stop picking up trapped cats from residents or shelter hours are reduced, cat intake may decline. But to the extent these factors remain constant over time, lower intake strongly suggests declining numbers of free-roaming cats.

Complaint calls are another indirect metric on the effect of targeting. It is possible any initial drop in volume will be due more to the positive behavioral impacts of spay/neuter rather than fewer cats. If the decline in complaints is sustained over time, that would suggest new, unaltered cats are not being born and replacing existing cats who pass away, resulting in a lower population. Requests for assistance in helping the cats, as opposed to complaints about them, are likely to spike upwards at the start of a targeted TNR effort as more people become aware services are available. As the project proceeds, the requests, too, should drop once most of the cats are sterilized.

Creative people have also tracked data such as the number of free kitten ads posted in local newspapers or online, the number of calls about stray cats to the town's sole veterinarian, the percentage of eartipped cats sighted in an area or an annual count of the number of cats who show up at a feeding station over the course of the same week. One idea is to review the data that helped identify the target area as a hot spot in the first place and use the same statistics or information to measure impact.

TNR programs that have enough bandwidth can track a combination of direct and indirect metrics. They can ask each assisted caretaker to regularly report on their colony's size. Cumulating these results can provide valuable information. If the overall number of colony cats being tracked in the target area is decreasing at the same time intake is going down, it reinforces the inference the free-roaming population is in decline.

In evaluating metrics, it is informative to compare the results in the target area to those outside that area over the same time period. This will give a truer picture of the impact of the project. If intake from the target area was flat the year before the project began compared to the year after it was completed, it might be tempting to conclude the effort had no effect. However, if during the same intervals, intake in the rest of the service area went up 10%, the exact opposite conclusion could be drawn.

One interesting observation PetSmart Charities made in reviewing data reported for targeted grant projects was how quickly impact appeared. The expectation at first was that any impact would not be evident for at least a year or two after a project ended. To the contrary, improvement in metrics such as intake and complaint calls often occurred during the projects themselves, showing how powerful the strategy can be.

Micro-targeting

Within a target area, there may be types of locations where free-roaming cats are more likely to be found in higher numbers than elsewhere. These kinds of places often have large, easily accessible food sources and can include apartment complexes, shopping centers, business districts (especially if they have many restaurants), mobile home parks and landfills. Parks can be home to large colonies, too, because of the abundant shelter. Focusing on these kinds of locations within a target area, because of their relatively high cat populations, can be an effective tactic.

Including owned cats

Within the area targeted, there are also likely to be unaltered cats who spend their time strictly indoors. In low-income areas, more indoor cats will tend to be unsterilized than in more prosperous locations. If resources are available, it makes good sense to get these cats spayed or neutered along with the free-roamers. Today's unaltered indoor pet can become tomorrow's free-roaming intact cat, so getting as many pet cats in the area sterilized as possible will help protect gains made from the TNR work. This also takes advantages of efficiencies — program and staff are already in the area and making contact with community members. It will be less work to spay or neuter all the cats while staff are there rather than come in once to do TNR, then come back another time to spay or neuter indoor pets.

Programs may learn about these indoor cats in the normal course of events — a caretaker with a colony may mention she also has a pet cat at home who needs to be sterilized. Residents may come up to a wrapped vehicle or program staff and inquire about services for their pets. Projects can also be proactive and indicate in marketing materials that all cats, owned and unowned, indoor and out, are eligible for the program.

Planning for follow up

The purpose of targeting — both colonies and sections of a community — is to make a big enough dent in the unaltered population that the total population numbers start going down. The intervention by itself, however, is not the complete solution. While the bulk of the work is done after a substantial percentage of the targeted cat population is spayed or neutered, progress needs to be maintained over time. Cats and colonies who were missed need to be TNR'd eventually — the sooner the better — even if the pace at which they are captured and sterilized is slower than the initial targeted effort. Abandonment will not end because the free-roaming cats are sterilized, so caretakers need to be alert to contact the TNR program and report any newcomers. While the target area will require fewer resources after completing intensive targeting, some ongoing level of attention will be required to ensure the population continues to drop.

Targeting case studies

Much has been learned from those who have received PetSmart Charities' free-roaming cat spay/neuter grants. The pitfalls and issues grantees faced and the ways they overcame them have informed much of the material in this guide. In addition, the data collected demonstrates how impactful and life-saving targeting can be when it is done effectively.

Brownwood, Texas
Corrine T. Smith Animal Center and PetSmart Charities

The Corrine T. Smith Animal Center (aka Brown County Humane Society) operates an open admission shelter in the small, rural Texas town of Brownwood. The only shelter in Brown County (pop. 38,000), it also serves several adjoining rural counties. Cat overpopulation in the community is severe — in 2010, the shelter took in over 2,100 cats and euthanized close to 90%. In June, 2011, they received a grant from PetSmart Charities to do targeted TNR in Brownwood, the county seat with a population of approximately 19,000.

Shelter staff and volunteers trapped cats in public areas. In addition, the shelter gave spay/neuter vouchers to local residents who caught cats themselves on their properties and brought them for surgery at a local veterinarian. When people trapped feral and stray cats and brought them to the shelter for surrender, shelter staff would ask if they would take them back if the cats were spayed or neutered and many agreed to do so. In a little over a year and a half, finishing in early 2013, 738 cats were sterilized. Cat intake to the group's shelter went from 2,117 cats in 2010 to 1,520 in 2012, a 28% decline, and cat euthanasia from 1,868 to 1,181, a 37% decline, with almost all the gains coming in the year after the project began (Figure 13).

Figure 13. **Cat intake and euthanasia: Corrine T. Smith Animal Center**

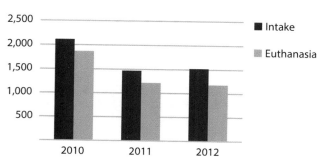

Tampa, Fla.
Humane Society of Tampa Bay and PetSmart Charities

The Humane Society of Tampa Bay (HSTB) has, since 2007, developed one of the strongest community TNR programs in the United States. They operate a limited admission shelter and high-volume spay/neuter clinic and became one of the first organizations to hire a full-time community cats coordinator. HSTB offers heavily discounted spay/neuter surgeries to caretakers registered in their online colony database, which now includes thousands of colonies throughout Hillsborough County. They have a feral cat patio adjoining their clinic where select trappers can drop off cats at any time, run a no-fee trap bank and are advocates for progressive government policies on free-roaming cats.

In July 2010, with funding from PetSmart Charities, HSTB launched their first targeted TNR project, choosing ZIP code 33612, which was the second highest ZIP code for cat intake to the open admission county shelter, Hillsborough County Animal Services. Known as "Suitcase City" because of its large transient population, 33612 is a low-income community with many mobile home parks and apartment complexes and about 45,000 residents. The goal was to alter 3,600 free-roaming cats in two years with HSTB's community cats coordinator leading the effort and organizing volunteer trappers. Using the "divide human population by six" formula recommended at that time, the group estimated there were approximately 7,500 free-roaming cats in 33612.

The group took a very methodical approach, working its way through the ZIP code block by block. Outreach took a number of forms in addition to their constant face-to-face presence in the community. The vehicle devoted to the project was wrapped in a way to draw attention and many resident caretakers would approach the van to provide information on their cats' whereabouts. The group also posted a billboard at a strategic intersection, and people would often stop to take a photo of it so they could call the number later. When calls slowed, HSTB

placed yard signs throughout the area. These outreach materials were similar to those used by HSTB in a subsequent ZIP code project. At a later point during the 33612 project, HSTB realized their original estimate of the number of cats was too high and they began to run out of cats. Trapping was then expanded into an adjoining ZIP code.

By the end of the project in September, 2012, 2,920 cats had been TNR'd in ZIP code 33612. Comparing 2013 to 2009, the full calendar year before the project started, cat intake to the county shelter from 33612 had dropped 47% (Figure 14a). This compared favorably to a 17% decline in all other areas of the county over the same time period (Figure 14b).

Cat intake: Hillsborough County Animal Services

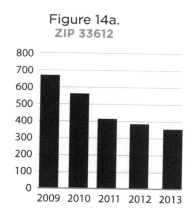

Figure 14a.
ZIP 33612

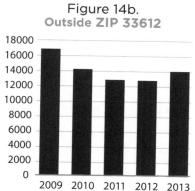

Figure 14b.
Outside ZIP 33612

Haywood County, N.C.
Haywood Animal Welfare Association, Humane Alliance and PetSmart Charities

This group provides rescue and spay/neuter services to Haywood County, a rural county of 59,000 people spread over 555 square miles. The group began its targeted TNR project in July 2010, supported by a free-roaming cat spay/neuter grant from PetSmart Charities. The project focused initially on 96 mobile home parks located in four of the county's towns. The targeted mobile home parks collectively accounted for more than half the cat intake to the open admission Haywood County Animal Shelter. Volunteers made an effort to get to know residents of the parks, assisting them with multiple animal-related needs, such as eliminating fleas and sealing off areas where cats were not desired. A goal was to identify a key park resident or two who could be a point person for the TNR process. The Humane Alliance provided transport to and from their spay/neuter clinic in Asheville, N.C.

Figure 15. **Cat intake and euthanasia: Haywood County Animal Shelter**

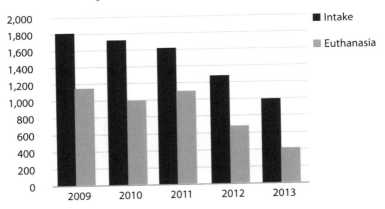

About halfway through the original two-year grant period, as the logistics of working in mobile home parks was proving a slow process, Haywood Animal Welfare Association expanded the target area to include the four towns themselves. The main form of outreach was door-to-door canvassing. Funding for the project was later provided for an additional two years and the target area expanded again, this time to the entire county. By the end of 2013, 1,897 free-roaming cats had been altered. Cat intake at the county shelter, comparing 2013 to 2009, was down 45% while euthanasia dropped 64% (Figure 15).

Louisville, Ky.
Alley Cat Advocates, Metro Animal Service and PetSmart Charities

Alley Cat Advocates formed in 1999 to advance TNR in the Louisville region. Their original focus was on organizing high-volume spay days for feral cats trapped by caretakers. These one-day clinics made it possible to sterilize large numbers of cats quickly and cost-efficiently. Looking to increase their impact, the group launched a targeted TNR project at the start of 2010 with a grant from PetSmart Charities. The project focused on one Louisville ZIP code (40215), which accounted for the highest cat intake to Metro Animal Services, the city's open admission shelter. The ZIP code is a low-income urban community covering close to four square miles with a population around 22,000. Using the "divide the human population by six" formula then in use, the group estimated there were close to 3,700 free-roaming cats in 40215. The group received funding for 2,000 surgeries over a period of two years.

Early on, the group found there were not as many caretakers as expected willing to trap and transport, so Alley Cat Advocates had to devote more of their own volunteers' time to field work. One method they used to find colonies was to take stray cats surrendered to Metro Animal Services from 40215 and, after spaying or neutering, return them to their original locations.

Under the theory that where there had been one intact free-roaming cat there were likely more, they would canvas the return locations for other cats to TNR. Another innovation involved Alley Cat Advocates volunteers riding along when Metro Animal Services officers responded to cat-related complaint calls from ZIP code 40215. Together, the volunteers and officers assessed whether it was practical to TNR the cat in question and keep her where she was rather than automatically bringing her into the shelter.

After a year and a half, the group had altered approximately 800 cats and was having difficulty locating more. During the time they'd been working, intake from the target ZIP code was dropping at a rate faster than the rest of the shelter's service area. At that point, the group concluded there were far fewer cats in the target area than originally estimated and decided to expand into two adjoining ZIP codes. After an additional 550 surgeries were performed, there was a significant drop in intake in the two new ZIP codes as well. The group again expanded the target area to add seven more ZIP codes so the grant's goal of 2,000 surgeries could be met in a timely manner. After the original grant ended, PetSmart Charities provided additional funding and the TNR work continued in ZIP code 40215 and others.

Intake from the original target ZIP code of 40215 declined 58% when comparing 2013 to 2009, the year before the project began (Figure 16a). In the rest of the shelter's service area, cat intake dropped 39% during that same time period (Figure 16b).

The impact of the Alley Cat Advocates TNR project went well beyond shelter data. The city council member whose district included ZIP code 40215 saw a noticeable drop in the volume of complaint calls to her office about stray and unowned cats and she credited the TNR program. She advocated for TNR with other council members and the result was an ordinance that directed Metro Animal Services to develop a Trap-Neuter-Return program.

Cat intake: Metro Animal Services

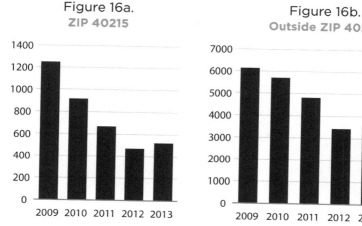

Figure 16a.
ZIP 40215

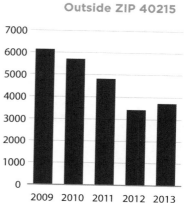

Figure 16b.
Outside ZIP 40215

The ordinance exempted caretakers from licensing and other requirements imposed on pet owners and created other legal protections for community cats. In addition, the Return to Field program begun in ZIP code 40215 by Alley Cat Advocates, dubbed Operation City Kitty, was expanded to include all healthy but unadoptable free-roaming cats brought to the city shelter. The animal control officer ride-along program was similarly expanded and formally named Operation Save-A-Life.

With a Return to Field program, instead of being euthanized, the cat is spayed, vaccinated and eartipped. After a night or two of recovery time, she is transported back to her original location and released.

5.
Return to Field

What is Return to Field?

A typical Return to Field is depicted in Figure 17. A free-roaming cat is trapped by a private citizen or animal control officer and brought to the local open admission shelter. Although the cat is perfectly healthy, she is feral and unadoptable. Even if she was friendly, the shelter may have no space or foster homes to hold her. The traditional practice in these circumstances is to euthanize the cat after any mandatory holding period. With a Return to Field program, instead of being euthanized, the cat is spayed, vaccinated and eartipped. After a night or two of recovery time, she is transported back to her original location and released.

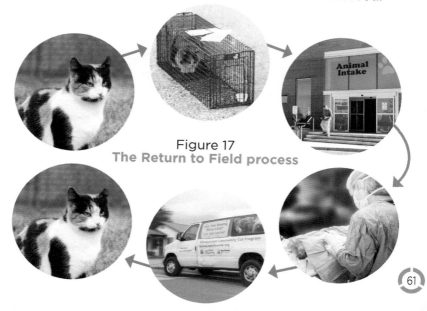

Figure 17
The Return to Field process

Why do Return to Field?

Return to Field is a recent innovation, born of the realization that euthanasia is an ineffective approach to managing free-roaming cat populations. Shelters that routinely euthanize large numbers of cats rarely see intake or complaint calls drop over time as a result, and instead are normally faced with steady or rising levels.

With respect to free-roaming cats, there are several reasons why euthanasia fails to curb their numbers:

Too many cats, too few animal control resources.
The population of free-roaming cats in most communities is too high when compared to the available animal control resources. There is little if any chance of trapping and euthanizing enough cats to make a dent in their population. As a result, animal control typically does not make any sustained, systematic attempt to remove cats, but at the most only responds to random complaints from residents. From a population control perspective, these efforts are no more than token in nature and have little effect.

Caretaker resistance. People who feed cats regularly form a bond to them and are protective. They will usually not cooperate with trapping when they know the outcome will be the cats' deaths. Passive resistance can include withholding crucial information like the cats' numbers and habits. More active resistance can involve feeding the cats prior to trapping attempts, so cats are not hungry enough to go into the traps. Some resistant caretakers may set traps off when no one is watching. For any population control program to be successful, caretakers must be on board — one reason TNR can work when trapping and euthanizing cannot.

Vacuum effect. This occurs when a colony of cats is completely removed from a location, but the food source and shelter remain. A vacuum is created and before long, other cats in the area move in to take advantage of the resources. If the cats are intact, the colony will grow right back to the level the available resources can support. This phenomenon was first documented by a wildlife biologist studying London street cats.[11]

Failure to capture all colony members. It is common for animal control not to catch all the cats at a specific location. The time officers can devote to trapping is limited, they may not even know how many cats are present and some cats are very hard to catch. When all the members of a colony are not captured, those left behind have less competition for the available resources and more of their offspring are likely to survive. Once again, it is not long before the number of cats rises to match what the environment can support.

The public opposes euthanasia. In 2007, a Harris poll sponsored by Alley Cat Allies surveyed public opinion on lethal control of community cats. More than 70% of respondents believed it was more humane to leave stray cats where they are rather than euthanize them, even if the cats would only live for two years.[12]

Constantly high levels of euthanasia carry a significant price for a shelter. There are financial costs, which may include staff time spent trapping, transporting or caring for the cats during any required holding periods. The shelter also must cover costs for fuel, food, litter, euthanasia procedures and the disposal of the bodies. Then there are the emotional costs. When shelters become places where large numbers of cats die on almost a daily basis, the stress on staff can be intense,

---

[11] R, Tabor, "The Wild Life of the Domestic Cat," Arrow Books (1983).

[12] K. Chu and W. Anderson, "U.S. Public Opinion on Humane Treatment of Stray Cats," Law & Policy Brief, Alley Cat Allies (2007).

5. Return to Field

resulting in low job satisfaction and high turnover. There is also potential damage to the shelter's public image. Even though the perception may not always be fair, many people view agencies associated with high levels of euthanasia in a negative light. After many years of bearing these costs from high cat euthanasia and seeing no improvement, shelters have begun to look for a better way, leading to the growing popularity of Return to Field.

Return to Field challenges traditional concepts of what is humane. Many people have a hard time accepting the fact that it is a better outcome for the cats to be sterilized and released to their original locations than euthanized. Probably the best proponents of Return to Field as a humane practice are the cats themselves. The ones eligible for return come into the shelter healthy, based on their appearance and body weight. It can be reasonably inferred they are doing sufficiently well in their environment and have adequate food and shelter, even if the source of these resources is unknown. It is difficult to see how ending a cat's life would be more humane than putting him back where he was doing well, with the added benefits of having him now sterilized and vaccinated.

Of course there are risks for any animal who is free-roaming and living outdoors. The widespread adoption of TNR programs has increased awareness that, despite these risks, community cats can lead quality lives. In a study of over 100,000 cats treated at TNR clinics over the course of 11 years, less than half of one percent had to be euthanized due to poor health.[13]

One objection sometimes voiced is the cats were brought to the shelter because someone did not want them around. Bringing them back to their original locations creates a heightened risk they will be harmed by the people who complained. So far, this fear has not been realized by shelters with Return to Field programs in cities such as Jacksonville, Fla.; San Antonio,

---

[13] Wallace and Levy, Journal of Feline Medicine and Surgery 8, 279–284.

Texas; San Jose, Calif.; and Albuquerque, N.M. In most jurisdictions, there are laws against animal cruelty and the great majority of people will not act violently against the cats, even if they disagree with the policy of returning them. In addition, the returned cats are spayed or neutered. For these cats at least, behaviors that may have led to the complaints about noise, odor and litters of kittens in the first place are largely eliminated.

Benefits

An immediate and often dramatic reduction in euthanasia is the most direct benefit of Return to Field. Every cat released is one less euthanized. In addition, by moving cats who will be returned to field in and out of the shelter quickly, cats who are being held at the facility for adoption are exposed to less disease and overcrowding, reducing euthanasia among these cats for medical reasons. As shelters increasingly define themselves as agencies designed to save lives, not end them, Return to Field can go a long way towards helping them realize this goal.

Resources once spent capturing, holding and euthanizing cats can be put into life-saving programs, including Return to Field, discount spay/neuter for low income families, foster programs and adoptions. How much is available for reallocation will vary according to each shelter's former practices. Those who in the past regularly sent animal control officers out to trap cats in response to citizen complaints will save the most as these officers can instead use their time for more productive purposes.

Return to Field can also change a shelter's culture. To see animals who normally were condemned the moment they entered the facility instead leave alive can be highly motivating and energizing for staff. Many shelter staff members were originally drawn to their positions out of a desire to help animals, and an alternative to euthanasia can relieve stress and offer them a deeper sense of fulfillment.

The perception of the shelter in the community can change, too. It is no longer the "pound," an unpleasant place associated with large numbers of cats dying, but somewhere cats are saved and protected. The more positive image can lead to improved fundraising and, as more people become interested and willing to visit and support the shelter, higher adoption rates.

Another possible benefit from Return to Field is a reduction in cat intake. Some agencies, including Jacksonville[14] and San Jose,[15] experienced this soon after launching a Return to Field program. Why intake dropped in these shelters is a matter of some dispute. There are those who believe these declines reflected a falling free-roaming cat population in those communities, caused by the spaying or neutering of the cats being returned. But as discussed earlier, unless targeting is part of the strategy, reduction in a community's population of free-roaming cats through spay/neuter cannot be achieved.

In the first years of Return to Field in Jacksonville and San Jose, no targeting was performed. The release of a cat to his original location was essentially the end of the process. Door hangers or other materials explaining the program may have been distributed in the neighborhood, but no attempts were necessarily made to locate and TNR other cats in the same area. If the returned cat was part of a 10-cat colony, he might end up being the only altered member (Figure 18). In that case, no population control would result because the remaining reproductive capacity in the nine unaltered cats would more than compensate for the loss in the one returned.

When a Return to Field program lacks any element of targeting, the absence of population control can also be seen on the community level. Because Return to Field

---

[14] See Figure 27.

[15] San Jose Animal Care & Services' Return to Field program launched in March of 2010. In 2012, cat intake was down 29% compared to 2009 (from 11,839 to 8,370). Euthanasia during the same period dropped 67% (from 8,466 to 2,799).

Figure 18. Return to Field with no colony-level targeting

cats originate from and are returned throughout the shelter's service area, the impact of their spay/neuter surgeries is randomly distributed (Figure 19). With surgeries not being concentrated either in individual colonies or sections of the community, overall reproductive capacity does not decrease anywhere in a meaningful way.

Figure 19. Community view: Return to Field with no colony-level targeting

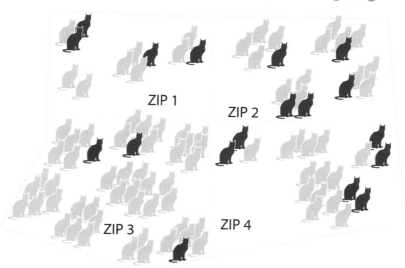

If not a falling free-roaming cat population, what then accounts for the drops in intake observed in Jacksonville and San Jose? Theoretically, there could have been factors at play that were completely unrelated to the Return to Field programs. However, the agencies involved have not identified any other significant new programs or changes in shelter policy that could have been expected to materially impact cat intake around the time the Return to Field projects got underway.

If the drops in intake were related to Return to Field, as seems probable, possible causes include discouragement of trapping by volume trappers as well as ordinary citizens, and a new perception that free-roaming cats are a valid part of the community.

Many communities have "volume trappers" — individuals or private extermination companies responsible for trapping and surrendering a disproportionate number of cats to local open admission shelters. Private companies are motivated by profit while individuals may be motivated for ideological reasons, such as the belief cats are better off euthanized than living on the streets. A Return to Field program effectively shuts down these activities. Residents won't hire a company to remove cats and ideologically driven individuals will not trap volumes of cats for euthanasia at the shelter if it is known the cats are going to be returned right back to where they were captured. Likewise, for the same reason, a resident looking to remove a few cats in his backyard will have to find a different solution than surrendering them at the shelter.

Return to Field also helps redefine the community's relationship to free-roaming cats. The common practice of euthanasia sends the message that free-roaming cats don't belong where they are and their lives are worth so little that rendering death is acceptable when there are no other placement options. With Return to Field, the community is taught that free-roaming cats do have lives of value and, if they are spayed or neutered and vaccinated, they become an acceptable part of the environment. This may cause fewer residents to consider bringing outdoor cats to the shelter. Some may even be inspired to get cats in their neighborhood sterilized, too.

The impact these cultural factors may have on decreasing cat intake is likely to occur mostly in the years immediately after the introduction of a Return to Field program. The discouragement of volume trappers and private extermination companies will be a one-time gain — their valve to the shelter can only be turned off once. Acceptance of free-roaming cats will be a slower process, but after most of the community is comfortable with their presence, further reductions in intake because of this new attitude could be minimal.

It is also possible cultural factors may not result in a drop in intake at all, at least not right away. While Jacksonville and San Jose saw drops in cat intake at the start of their programs, San Antonio had the opposite experience.

On April 1, 2012, San Antonio Animal Care Services launched a Return to Field program covering 14 ZIP codes in the City of San Antonio as part of a joint project with Best Friends Animal Society and PetSmart Charities. Named the Community Cats Project, the program combined Return to Field with targeted TNR. Almost immediately, cat intake from the target area shot up, increasing 69% in 2012 compared to 2011 (Figure 20).

Figure 20. Cat intake and euthanasia: San Antonio Animal Care Services

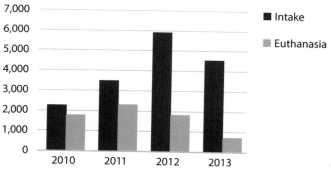

There were a few possible reasons for this. Dog intake into the shelter had in the past been disproportionately high compared to cat intake, a possible sign that cat overpopulation had largely been ignored by the community. The advent of the Community Cats Project raised awareness of free-roaming cats and residents starting taking action, including bringing large numbers of cats and especially litters of kittens to the shelter. The new perception of the shelter as a cat-friendly facility that would not euthanize may have further encouraged this activity. While the exact causes of the rapid rise in intake may not be fully known, San Antonio shows how circumstances will vary from community to community and highlights how the impact of Return to Field on intake can be unpredictable.

At the same time, San Antonio's experience demonstrates the power of Return to Field to reduce euthanasia. Despite the large spike in intake, the number of cats euthanized in 2012 from the target ZIP codes actually decreased 21% from the prior year (from 2,312 to 1,828), resulting in the live release rate for target-area cats almost doubling from 31% to 61%. In 2013, euthanasia continued to decline, falling to 740 cats, a 68% drop compared to 2011. In addition, intake in 2013 began sharply falling back down (Figure 20) and the live release rate for the target ZIP codes rose to 72%.

If the goal is to improve conditions not only for cats in the shelter, but for all the residents and cats in the community, Return to Field alone is not enough to achieve that goal.

Limitations

There are major limitations on what can be accomplished when Return to Field is the only significant TNR-related program being performed in a community. As discussed, Return to Field alone does not reduce the population of free-roaming cats because it is not at all targeted. While the shelter will benefit from lower euthanasia and perhaps decreased intake, the community as a whole will still have to deal with just as large an overpopulation of cats. If the goal is to improve conditions not only for cats in the shelter, but for all the residents and cats in the community, Return to Field alone is not enough to achieve that goal.

Sustainability is also a concern with a stand-alone Return to Field program. The free-roaming cat population is the source of the cats who enter a shelter and are then returned outside. If that population never goes down, then theoretically neither will the number of cats needing to be returned. Running a Return to Field program requires a substantial amount of resources, including surgeries, transportation and staff. If the volume of cats returned remains constant, year after year, the same level of resources will have to be committed indefinitely. This could prove difficult for many shelters and their partners to maintain.

The way to address these issues is by making Return to Field an important part of a community TNR program, but not the only element. Concurrently employing other tactics such as targeting and grassroots mobilization will allow a community to gain the benefits of Return to Field while also getting to the heart of the matter — reducing the number of cats out on the streets.

Combining Return to Field and targeting

In a stand-alone Return to Field program, only the shelter cat being released is spayed or neutered (Figure 18). If colony-level targeting is incorporated into Return to Field, the impact can be much greater. If a high enough percentage of cats is caught and treated with follow-up TNR (Figure 21), population decline is now possible at that location. In addition, the colony will be all or mostly vaccinated and nuisance behavior will abate.

Figure 21. **Return to Field with colony-level targeting**

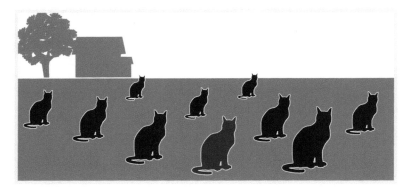

Because cats being returned to field originate from throughout a shelter's service area, integrating colony-level targeting alone will result in scattered colonies being TNR'd (Figure 22). While overall population decline is possible using this approach, adding community-level targeting to the mix will make for a more efficient use of resources and faster population reduction.

In Figure 23, the same cats are returned to field as in Figure 22 and the same number of surgeries performed on non-shelter cats. But instead of targeting colonies of returned cats, colonies in ZIP code 3 are targeted, whether they include a Return to Field cat or not. By concentrating all the non-shelter cat surgeries in one section of the community, the program significantly reduced the possibility of migration of unaltered cats

Figure 22. **Community view: Return to Field with colony-level targeting**

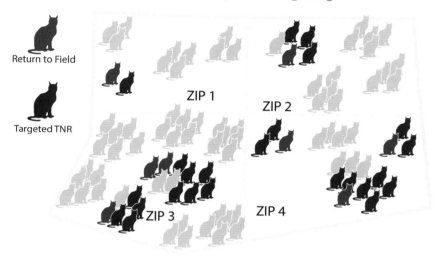

Figure 23.
Return to Field plus community-level targeting

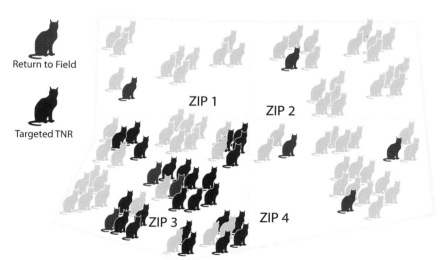

into TNR'd colonies and accelerated population decline. TNR programs may also find it more practical and efficient to target sections of a community rather than every colony of every cat returned to field. There will be economies of scale in terms of staff time, transportation and outreach by focusing resources in one area. If there are not enough surgeries available, anyway, to effectively target all returned cats' colonies, community-level targeting makes even more sense.

The strategy depicted in Figure 23 does have an inefficiency. The surgeries of the cats returned to field outside ZIP code 3 are not contributing to population reduction because no other cats in their colonies are being altered. To avoid this inefficiency, the program could target a section of the community and only return to field shelter cats from that selected area.

In Figure 24, instead of returning five shelter cats to ZIP codes 1, 2 and 4, as was done in Figure 23, these surgeries are allocated to an additional colony in ZIP code 3 (green).

Figure 24.
Return to Field only in community-level target area

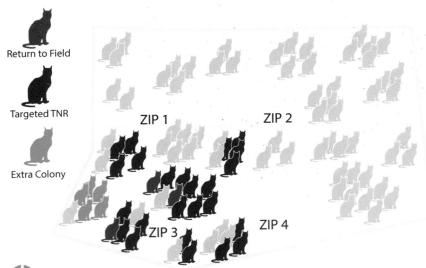

Return to Field

Targeted TNR

Extra Colony

ZIP 1

ZIP 2

ZIP 3

ZIP 4

By concentrating all available spays and neuters in ZIP code 3, the program can achieve the greatest potential for population decline from these surgeries and other TNR resources, such as staff time and transportation.

While limiting Return to Field to a target area may be the most efficient and fastest method for reducing the number of community cats, other considerations weigh against this approach. It can be stressful for shelter staff if cats otherwise eligible for being returned to field are euthanized only because they do not originate from the target area. Limiting the number of returned cats will also reduce improvement in euthanasia numbers and lessen other benefits of a Return to Field program. These factors may support a decision to return all eligible cats and accept a degree of inefficiency when it comes to population control.

When combining Return to Field with targeted TNR, the same agency does not need to perform both tactics. The shelter may use its own staff and resources to alter and return eligible shelter cats while a local TNR nonprofit does follow-up trapping in the returned cats' colonies or targets a high-intake area. Or each agency may perform different parts of each tactic. However the roles are assigned, what is critical is to have a coordinated strategy on the community level.

However the roles are assigned, what is critical is to have a coordinated strategy on the community level.

Mechanics

The importance of timing

The day-to-day details of managing a Return to Field program will vary widely depending on available resources, local ordinances and policies, and agency preferences. But one guideline that will always be applicable is the need to move the cats through the process expeditiously. The goal is not to rush them through and cut corners. As long as a proper level of care is provided, the faster the cats are out of the shelter, altered and returned to the field, the better. This reduces crowding and lessens the occurrence of upper respiratory infections and other stress-induced illnesses among the shelter's general cat population.

Municipal support

When a community is used to seeing a shelter as a place to dispose of cats considered nuisances, Return to Field represents a dramatic shift in the opposite direction. It can be reasonably expected there will be complaints from some about the new policy. There are also special interest groups that have traditionally opposed anything to do with TNR, and Return to Field will be no exception.

All relevant agencies and officials in the local government should anticipate resistance and agree upon a uniform message in response. One messaging option is that the past practice of euthanizing free-roaming cats has failed to make any progress and Return to Field is now the policy. Ideally, all callers or complainants should be referred to the same agency or person for the official response. If all parties in the government

> As long as a proper level of care is provided, the faster the cats are out of the shelter, altered and returned to the field, the better.

are not on the same page, program opponents could try to exploit this to build resistance to the program. It is critical to educate relevant officials and gain approval prior to the program's launch. If the possibility of an amplified level of criticism is a concern, it may be helpful to wait until there is demonstrable success before going to the media and broadly announcing the program.

Program planners also need to carefully examine and, if necessary, seek amendments to existing ordinances to ensure a Return to Field program is legally compliant. This may include reviewing laws on animals being at large, licensing requirements, pet limits and outdoor feeding bans.

Intake procedures

Free-roaming cats may end up at a shelter by various means. Animal control officers may trap them or pick up cats captured by residents. Residents themselves may bring cats in, using their own traps, carriers or, with friendly cats and young kittens, their own arms. However it occurs, it is essential at the point of intake to gather as much information about the cat as possible. If the cat may be returned to field, details about the location of the cat's territory are vital. In order to assess eligibility, information about the cat's lifestyle is also needed — was this a family pet? A cat who lived strictly indoors? Are there any known underlying medical issues? This data should be recorded and a copy attached to the trap or cage confining the cat. The record should always then accompany the cat throughout the Return to Field process.

One policy issue to resolve in advance is whether residents surrendering cats should be informed about the Return to Field program. If intake staff is upfront about the fact the cat might be coming back, this could provoke a confrontation, resulting in stressful, heated discussion and wasted time. On the other hand, some people will be glad to have the cat returned, knowing he will now be sterilized and vaccinated. As long as there is no legal obligation to disclose, this is a decision for each agency to make and possibly adjust as experience is gained. One option to consider is including language in the shelter's surrender form. The form can reserve the right of the shelter to determine the cat's disposition, including sterilizing the cat and returning him to his original territory. This provides notice a cat may be brought back and may reduce complaints if and when that happens.

Eligibility criteria

A primary justification for Return to Field is that the cats being returned were doing well in their environment at the time of intake and it is more humane to put them back than end their lives. This principle does not apply to cats who are sick, malnourished, injured or declawed. It also excludes cats who were strictly indoor pets and never lived outdoors or kittens too young to survive on their own.

A shelter may decide to put other limitations on eligibility for Return to Field. Some agencies may choose to only return true ferals and not sociable cats, on the belief friendly cats are too much at risk and do not belong outdoors. Others will take the opposite position and decide to return any healthy outdoor cat who would otherwise be euthanized. In time, a Return to Field program may create enough cage space and healthier conditions at the shelter so that there is no need to return friendly cats to field. Instead, they can be held for adoption. Until that point is reached, one thing to consider is that some friendly, free-roaming cats turned into the shelter may actually be pets allowed outdoors by their owners. If returned to field, they may simply find their own way back home.

Another matter of discretion is the minimum age for a kitten to be released. In Louisville, the Return to Field program operated by Metro Animal Services and Alley Cat Advocates has a strict age requirement of four months. If kittens are younger, they can only be returned to field if an identified caretaker agrees to the return at the exact address they originated from and is present at the time of the return. Otherwise, alternate placements are sought. Interestingly, the program has found that the resident who brought the kittens to the shelter is often willing to take them back upon learning they will be spayed or neutered. This shows how sometimes community cats are brought to a shelter not because a resident dislikes having them around, but because she is concerned about the growth of their population and does not know of any other solution.

Other programs are more flexible, believing circumstances vary according to the exact age of the kittens. Possible guidelines include the following:

- Kittens less than 8 weeks are not eligible for release.

- Kittens between 8 to 12 weeks may be returned to field if a caretaker is identified and has agreed to the time and location of the release.

- Kittens between 12 to 16 weeks may be released at or very near the address where they were seized or colony site. Efforts should be made at the time of release to locate caretakers in the area.

- Kittens more than 16 weeks may be released within a reasonable distance of their original location, similar to adults.

The criteria decided upon for eligibility, including state of health, sociability and age, should be documented and treated as standard operating procedures.

Housing decisions and resources

The cats' eligibility for Return to Field should be evaluated as soon as they enter the shelter. If there is room at the facility, some cats may need to be held long enough to make an accurate determination of their adoptability. But any cats who will clearly be going back to the field should be isolated from the rest of the shelter population and transported as quickly as possible to the spay/neuter clinic. A separate room as a temporary holding area is ideal, making it easy for staff to quickly identify eligible cats and preventing overcrowding in the shelter's general population. The cats will also need to be held at least overnight following their surgeries. Most Return to Field programs release the cats the day after the surgery. This is an acceptable recovery time provided there are no evident complications. Holding the cats for two nights would be preferable, but may not be practical if the program is handling a high volume of cats.

Where the cats are held for recovery will depend on where the surgeries are being done and what partners are involved in the overall program. If the shelter uses its own in-house clinic, the same isolation area used on intake could be used for recovery. If using an outside spay/neuter provider, the clinic may have space to hold the cats overnight for pickup the next morning. If the shelter does not perform the actual return of the cats but transfers them to a third party for release, such as a local TNR group, then that group may have a holding space to keep the cats post-surgery.

It is not necessary to house the cats in cages if suitable traps and trap dividers are available. Cats, and especially ferals, do well confined in traps for periods of up to several days. The traps take up much less space and, with the proper techniques, feeding and cleaning is simple and quick.[16]

If any cats will be kept in cages, feral cat dens should be used. These are hard plastic carriers with sliding front doors and a port-hole side door. They are specifically designed for housing feral cats. The cat should first be transferred from the trap into the den by lining up the rear door of the trap with the front door of the den. Once the cat is in, the den can be placed inside the cage and

---

[16] See footnote 10, page 48.

its side door lifted open by sliding a yardstick or pole through the bars of the closed cage door. When the cat is inside the den, the side door can be closed in similar fashion. Dens or transfer cages are also useful when the cats are transported back to their territories for release.

Spay/neuter logistics

A Return to Field program places unique demands on a spay/neuter provider. There is the need, following intake, to move the cats to the clinic as soon as possible. It is also unpredictable how many cats will enter the shelter and require sterilization on any given day. The ideal choice is a clinic that can receive cats on an almost daily basis and be flexible in terms of volume.

An in-house shelter clinic might be best positioned to meet these needs and could offer other advantages as well. It can greatly reduce transportation time and expenses if the cats have only to be carried across the hallway instead of driven to an outside provider. Medical costs, including materials and veterinary staff, are often lower with in-house surgical suites.

If an outside provider is used, having a clinic that is able to hold the cats overnight after their surgeries can be a great benefit. This would save one leg of transport by eliminating the need to move the cats back to the shelter for recovery or to a separate holding space.

As always with TNR, the ability to sterilize large numbers of cats is key. To further this goal, programs should limit standard veterinary treatment to what is absolutely required, including spay/neuter surgery, rabies vaccination and eartipping. Other treatments such as medication for fleas, ear mites, worms or other parasites should be applied on an "as needed" basis but not as part of a standard package all cats receive. Testing for feline leukemia (FeLV) or feline immunodeficiency virus (FIV) should only be performed on cats who appear ill and require diagnosis, or are candidates for adoption. Microchipping, unless required by local ordinance, is also a luxury with relatively little benefit in this context compared to the costs.

Transportation strategies

Transport requirements will differ according to how the Return to Field program functions. If the spay/neuter facility and post-surgery housing are at the shelter, this will limit transport to when the cats are returned to their original locations and released. On the other extreme, it may be necessary to transport a cat after intake from the shelter to an outside spay/neuter clinic, from the clinic to a recovery space and finally from the recovery space to the release location. Streamlining the process can save time and expense.

Having a dedicated vehicle can also be very helpful and is essential if regularly handling large volumes of cats. A cargo van allows for easy moving of cats and traps in and out. When not being used directly for Return to Field, the vehicle could be available for TNR of non-shelter cats. Wrapping the van in colorful advertising, including clear contact information for the program, can be excellent publicity and assist with outreach.

Personnel planning

In terms of labor, cats will need to be evaluated upon intake, temporarily housed, brought to the spay/neuter provider, cared for overnight post-surgery and transported back to their territories. In a busy shelter handling a large volume of cats, these tasks will need to be performed on almost a daily basis.

When layering targeted TNR on top of Return to Field, it may become necessary to divide the two tactics among different personnel. The TNR of entire colonies requires outreach, planning and preparation in advance of the trapping. Then the handling of the cats afterwards can be time-consuming. These duties may be difficult for someone who also has to meet the daily demands of quickly moving Return to Field cats in and out of the shelter.

Release procedures

It is safe to release adult cats within a reasonable distance, such as two blocks, of where they were first captured. Cats will know their territory well enough to recognize where they are and locate their colony site, food source and shelter. To avoid issues with property owners, releases should take place in a nearby public area, such as an alleyway, park or sidewalk of a quiet street. The release should be delayed if there is imminent danger, such as a pack of dogs or an overly hostile and aggressive property owner. For safety purposes, people doing releases should always inform shelter staff of their whereabouts and be able to quickly call someone in authority, such as an animal control officer, if the situation requires further assistance.

Programs can also educate residents in the immediate neighborhood by distributing door hangers that explain what Return to Field is, make it clear the program is now official policy and inform anyone with questions whom to contact for further information. This kind of outreach is particularly useful if the program's strategy includes the TNR of other cats in the vicinity of the release location. In that case, the door hangers should also announce the availability of services to trap and alter remaining cats.

Fostering collaboration

There are many roles to play in a combined Return to Field/targeted TNR program. Some shelters may choose to perform the entire program using their own facilities, staff and volunteers, while others will want to partner with local spay/neuter clinics or TNR groups. Bringing all the players in the community together to form a common strategy and assign specific roles will hasten progress in lowering euthanasia and reducing the free-roaming cat population. One possible scenario is for the shelter to transport the cats to a high-volume spay/neuter clinic. After the clinic performs the surgeries, it can in turn, hand them over to a TNR group for release and follow-up trapping of the rest of the colony. Meanwhile, a partner humane society or rescue organization could take in and place friendly cats and kittens so they don't need to be returned. The more organizations can pool and coordinate resources, the stronger the program and its impact will be.

> Bringing all the players in the community together to form a common strategy and assign specific roles will hasten progress in lowering euthanasia and reducing the free-roaming cat population.

Return to Field case studies

Jacksonville, Fla.
Jacksonville Animal Care & Protective Services,
First Coast No More Homeless Pets,
Best Friends Animal Society
and PetSmart Charities

On August 1, 2008, the first large-scale Return to Field program in the United States was launched in Jacksonville. Popularly known as "Feral Freedom," the program came about when First Coast No More Homeless Pets (FCNMHP), a high-volume spay/neuter clinic in

Jacksonville, asked the city's animal control shelter to release eartipped feral cats intaked at the shelter back to their caretakers and colonies. Much to the surprise of FCNMHP, the agency — Jacksonville Animal Care & Protective Services (JACPS) — was willing to release not only eartipped cats, but all feral cats. FCNMHP agreed to administer the program and secured private funding, including a grant from Best Friends Animal Society.

Every day, twice a day, FCNMHP picked up eligible cats from JACPS and transported them to the First Coast clinic. The cats were spayed and neutered, usually the same day they arrived, and held at the clinic overnight. The next morning, FCNMHP transported the cats back to their locations of origin for release. In the immediate area of the release, they distributed informational door hangers. No attempt was made to TNR other cats at the release locations, making Feral Freedom a stand-alone Return to Field program.

In the beginning, only feral cats were eligible. When the agencies realized many friendly cats were being euthanized because they were barred from the program, they began to include them as well. At first, all the cats were microchipped in an effort to track whether any came to a bad end, a common fear with Return to Field initiatives. The program discontinued the microchipping when no evidence of mistreatment of returned cats turned up.

There was an immediate, profound and ongoing reduction of euthanasia at JACPS. In 2008, when Feral Freedom had been in effect for only five months, euthanasia declined 15% compared to the year before (Figure 25). In 2009, the drop in euthanasia compared to 2007 was 47% and by 2013, it was down 92%. The euthanasia rate, meaning the percentage of cats taken in who were euthanized, plummeted from 85% in 2007 to 13% in 2013.

Impact on intake was evident following Feral Freedom's first full calendar year of operation. In 2010, cat intake fell 22% compared to 2009. In the following two years, declines in intake at JACPS were much more modest, falling 4% year-over-year in 2011, then 2% in 2012 (Figure 25). The leveling off of intake in 2011 and 2012 and the lack of any targeting suggest the large reduction in cat intake in 2010 near the onset of Feral Freedom may have been caused by cultural factors, not a shrinking community cat population.

Figure 25. **Cat intake, euthanasia and Return to Field: Jacksonville Animal Care & Protective Services**

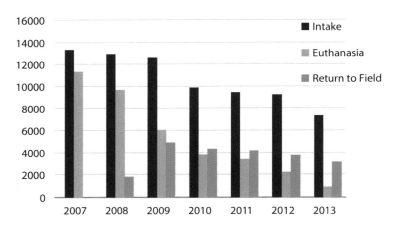

Most of the modest declines in intake which did occur in 2011 and 2012 may be attributed to a targeted spay/neuter project led by JACPS with strong support from FCNMHP and funded by PetSmart Charities. From early 2011 through June 2013, JACPS targeted one ZIP code in its service area, ZIP code 32210. At project completion, 1,688 community cats and 1,137 pet cats in the target area had been altered. Cat intake from ZIP code 32210 dropped by 51% in just two years (Figure 26). This reduction accounted for 74% of the drop in cat intake for the entire shelter in 2012 compared to 2010 (462 out of 625 fewer cats). The rapid, dramatic impact on intake from ZIP code 32210 likely reflected a declining community cat population in the target area.

Figure 26.
Cat intake from ZIP code 32210:
Jacksonville Animal Care & Protective Services

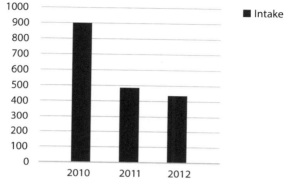

A substantial drop in intake occurred again in 2013 with intake falling 21% compared to the prior year (Figure 25). When Feral Freedom was launched in 2008, the local government changed its ordinances to legalize TNR in general. This, along with the publicity generated by Feral Freedom, led to a dramatic uptick in feral cat surgeries in the community at large, from just over 500 annually in 2008 to close to 11,000 per year by 2012. The significant volume of TNR activity by residents and local nonprofits may have impacted the size of the free-roaming cat population and been a factor behind the large intake drop seen in 2013.

With respect to the sustainability of the Feral Freedom program, an encouraging note is the number of cats returned to field consistently fell, from 4,917 in 2009 to 3,172 in 2013, a 35% decline. If the trajectory continues to go down and fewer cats need to be handled by Feral Freedom as time goes on, this will support the program's long-term viability. In addition, the municipality has recently set aside licensing revenue to help with the costs of the program. In this manner, the local government is returning some of the savings realized when FCNMHP took over the disposition of free-roaming cats.

The Jacksonville experience demonstrates the powerful impact a Return to Field program can have on euthanasia and potentially on intake as well. By layering targeting on top of Return to Field and mobilizing the public to perform TNR, the community also made progress in reducing its number of free-roaming cats.

Albuquerque, N.M.
Albuquerque Animal Welfare Department, Animal Humane New Mexico, New Mexico Animal Friends, Best Friends Animal Society and PetSmart Charities

In 2013, the Albuquerque Animal Welfare Department (AAWD) euthanized 1.1 cats per 1,000 residents in its service area, which includes the City of Albuquerque and remaining areas of Bernalillo County, N.M. This rate, one of the lowest among open admission shelters serving a major metropolitan area in the United States, was a dramatic reduction from the 7.7 euthanized cats per 1,000 residents by AAWD in 2010. This improvement in such a relatively short period was fueled almost entirely by a variety of community TNR tactics, including colony-level targeting, community-level targeting and Return to Field.

The groundwork for success was laid in 2008 when Animal Humane New Mexico, a private shelter, partnered with Street Cat Companions, the TNR program of New Mexico Animal Friends, to offer free spay/neuter surgeries for feral cats. Street Cat Companions used an entirely volunteer-run effort to target colonies throughout the city and county, achieving high sterilization rates within each colony and reaching most of the very large ones in the area. Also in 2008, AAWD suspended its trap rental program, which had been used primarily by residents to capture free-roaming cats and surrender them to the shelter.

In 2011, AAWD started its own Return to Field program, transferring surrendered ferals after they had been spayed or neutered to Street Cat Companions and other volunteer groups. These groups then released the cats back in their original locations. That same year Animal Humane New Mexico again partnered with Street Cat Companions to launch a TNR project targeting more than 2,000 cats in six ZIP codes surrounding its facility. This project, funded by grants from PetSmart Charities, was later expanded to include an additional ZIP code and over 2,000 more cats.

April 1, 2012, saw the advent of the Community Cats Project (CCP), a collaboration among AAWD, Best Friends Animal Society and PetSmart Charities. The idea behind the CCP was to build on the Feral Freedom model created in Jacksonville by integrating targeted TNR with Return to Field from the outset. Protocols called for not only returning cats to field, but then pursuing TNR of as many cats as possible at the release locations. Best Friends hired two staff members to work with AAWD and implement the program. On average, for every one cat returned to field, Best Friends TNR'd an additional three cats. The CCP was limited to the City of Albuquerque, but volunteers continued to also Return to Field cats who originated from elsewhere in Bernalillo County.

As a result of these programs, cat euthanasia at AAWD declined 85% in 2013 compared to 2010 and cat intake was down 28% (Figure 27). Over this period, the euthanasia rate fell from 53% to 11%. On average, 1,257 cats per year were returned to field from 2011 through 2013.

Figure 27. **Cat intake, euthanasia and Return to Field: Albuquerque Animal Welfare Department**

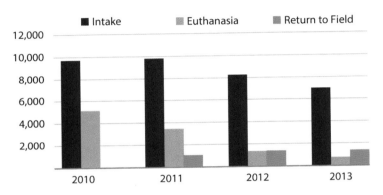

Similar to Jacksonville, the Return to Field component in Albuquerque was clearly the driving force behind the improvement in euthanasia. What caused intake to drop in 2012 and 2013 is less clear. Was it primarily cultural factors, as volume trappers were shut down and residents no longer viewed the shelter as a place to bring free-roaming cats? Or did targeting have as much or more of an impact by reducing the free-roaming cat population?

Intake dropping at a consistent rate two years in a row — down 16% in 2012 year-to-year, then again 16% in 2013, may reflect a declining free-roaming cat population, but it is too soon to say. The Return to Field program in San Jose, which lacks any element of targeting, saw intake decline consistently over the first three years of its implementation, though at an increasingly slower pace. It is also still unknown whether spaying or neutering three additional colony cats for every one cat returned to field is a sufficient ratio or whether many more non-shelter cats need to be altered to reduce the total free-roaming population.[17]

One clue may be provided by the colonies of returned cats being tracked by Best Friends. After the first year of the Community Cats Project, these 855 colonies contained 4,962 cats. The sterilization rate in these colonies averaged 77% and their total population had dropped by 4% since the start of the project. If the size of these colonies continues to decline along with intake, that might point to a shrinking free-roaming cat population being a significant driver behind the decreases in intake.

The impact on the number of community cats from the targeted TNR project by Animal Humane New Mexico is less in doubt. Animal Humane accepts all cats and kittens except ferals. Many of the kittens and friendly cats they take in originate from the free-roaming population. By the end of 2012, they had TNR'd approximately 2,000 cats and intake to their shelter from the six target ZIP codes was down 62%. Outside the target area, intake declined only 8% (Figure 28). The 351 fewer cats entering the shelter from the target area correlates closely to the 294 fewer cats euthanized at Animal Humane in 2012 compared to 2010.

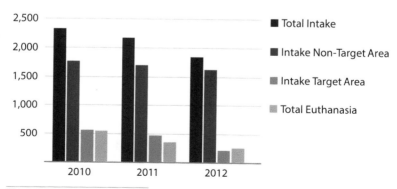

Figure 28. **Cat intake and euthanasia: Animal Humane New Mexico**

- Total Intake
- Intake Non-Target Area
- Intake Target Area
- Total Euthanasia

[17] Cat intake at San Jose Animal Care & Services went down 14% in 2010, the year its Return to Field program launched, compared to the prior year. Further year-to-year drops occurred of 11% in 2011 and 7% in 2012.

When cat intake and euthanasia at AAWD and Animal Humane — the two major shelters in Albuquerque — are combined, the community-wide trend of falling numbers in both categories is further evident (Figure 29). In 2013, compared to 2010, combined intake was down 27% and total euthanasia fell 84%.

Figure 29. Cat intake and euthanasia: Albuquerque Animal Welfare Department and Animal Humane New Mexico combined

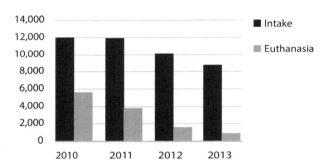

Another potential benefit of a Return to Field program is shown by AAWD's adoption numbers. On an absolute basis, the number of cats adopted by the agency was almost unchanged in 2013 compared to 2010, but as a percentage of intake, the rate gradually improved from 37% to 50% (Figure 30). This rise may reflect the improved overall health of shelter cats after the practice of admitting and holding ferals stopped. Due to the lack of crowding, AAWD could hold the cats longer until homes were found, and resources once allocated to euthanasia, could be used to enhance adoption programs.

Albuquerque also shows what can happen next when cat euthanasia is reduced to such low levels. By the end of 2012, after free-roaming cat euthanasia had practically ended at AAWD, there was an opportunity to explore why other cats were still being euthanized at the shelter.

Figure 30. **Cat intake and adoptions:**
Albuquerque Animal Welfare Department

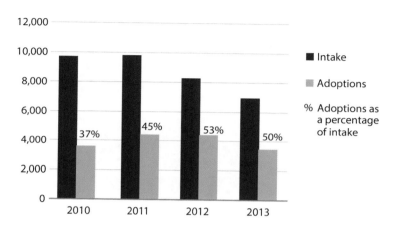

It was discovered that many of these cats were either orphaned newborn kittens or had contracted ringworm. Best Friends staffers and local volunteers established a new program to handle newborn kittens as well as isolation facilities to house cats with ringworm, contributing to further euthanasia declines at AAWD in 2013. At Animal Humane, a decline in kitten intake from their targeted project opened up a number of foster homes for adult cats with upper respiratory infections, who otherwise might have had no other housing.

Although it is uncertain exactly which elements of Albuquerque's community TNR program are responsible to what degree, the overall impact has been a tremendous reduction in euthanasia and significant drop in intake at local shelters. Once again, employing both Return to Field and targeting appears to be a potent combination.

One way to hasten progress is to use multiple tactics, such as grassroots mobilization and community-level targeting.

6.

Grassroots Mobilization

A TNR program can greatly expand its reach by mobilizing caretakers of community cat colonies and other interested residents to perform the bulk of the hands-on work of TNR themselves. For this tactic, the program and its personnel play a supportive role, providing the training, services and equipment needed for caretakers to do the job. Not only can more cats get altered when the public gets actively involved, but awareness of TNR and support for the method are increased.

In communities with very large populations of people and free-roaming cats, such as major cities, grassroots mobilization may be critical. Because there are so many cats, it might be unrealistic for a TNR program to expect its own staff and volunteers to capture enough cats to make much of a difference. On the other hand, in communities with relatively few residents and cats, it might not be necessary to mobilize the public. A handful of expert trappers could TNR enough cats faster and more easily. In most places, getting more people actively involved and contributing their time, effort and money will be advantageous, even if grassroots mobilization is not the program's primary tactic. If grassroots mobilization is the only tactic used, progress in reducing the community's free-roaming cat population may be slow and take a number of years, especially if there are thousands or tens of thousands of cats needing treatment. The slow pace may be due to resource constraints such as funds and limited availability of surgeries. In addition, not all caretakers will be motivated or physically able to TNR the cats they are feeding.

One way to hasten progress is to use multiple tactics, such as grassroots mobilization and community-level targeting. While caretakers throughout the service area work to get their colonies sterilized, the TNR program can use its own personnel to target high-need areas. This combination can achieve immediate population reduction in target sections while elsewhere a long-term drive proceeds towards fewer cats in the community.

Leadership

A grassroots TNR program can involve many players, including caretakers, veterinary clinics, shelters, animal control officers, rescue groups and expert trappers. The more services are coordinated and protocols standardized, the more effective the mobilization effort will be. For this to happen, there usually needs to be a leader responsible for the overall program. In the absence of clear leadership, the chances increase for needless duplication of some services and gaps in others. Conflicting information from multiple sources will also create confusion. These and other inefficiencies can blunt the impact of TNR in a community.

If multiple organizations are contributing to the grassroots effort, one agency can be the coordinator. Often the group most experienced with TNR can play this role, if it has the capacity to do so. If that capacity does not exist, it would be better to have another agency take the lead, relying on the more experienced group for counsel. What should be avoided are multiple agencies trying to take the lead in the same community. Competition can result not only in inefficiency but also a lack of dialogue and information-sharing, the exact opposite of the most desirable approach.

The lead agency can be responsible for several key aspects of the grassroots program, including:

- Developing curriculum for training
- Defining best practices
- Maintaining a website listing all TNR resources in the community
- Serving as the primary contact for inquiries from the public about TNR
- Identifying gaps in services
- Collecting data, such as colony locations and caretaker identities
- Reuniting eartipped cats turned into shelters with their caretakers and colonies
- Seeking funding
- Providing guidance to help TNR program participants remain in compliance with local laws.

What the lead agency should not try to do is dictate the roles of other participating organizations. Rather, it should meld together whatever resources agencies are willing to provide. To facilitate this, regularly scheduled meetings can be helpful.

If resources allow, hiring a community cats coordinator is an excellent step toward demonstrating professionalism and maximizing a program's impact.

The need for clearly defined leadership also exists within organizations making significant contributions to the grassroots effort. TNR has developed in the United States as a bottom-up movement, with individual caretakers and small nonprofits introducing and implementing the practice in their communities. As programs have grown larger and more sophisticated, the need has also grown to professionalize TNR and have dedicated staff. If resources allow, hiring a community cats coordinator is an excellent step toward demonstrating professionalism and maximizing a program's impact. Duties can include ensuring that:

- Calls and inquiries from the public get a timely response
- Trap banks are stocked and functioning
- Spay/neuter appointments are filled
- Volunteers are coordinated
- Transportation is arranged
- Bills are paid.

The lack of a specific staff member assigned these tasks can effectively limit the impact of a TNR program.

Training for caretakers

How much training is required for caretakers will depend on how much of the TNR process they will personally be responsible for performing. If their only role is to catch the cats, then all that might be needed is some in-field instruction. Topics to cover would include how to set and bait the traps, cover them up once a cat is inside and put traps in a safe place until program personnel come to transport cats. If caretakers are expected to perform the whole process — from scheduling spay/neuter appointments to caring for the cats post-surgery — far more extensive training at a formal workshop would be necessary.

The more caretakers do themselves, the more benefit accrues to the TNR program. But any TNR program's expectations of what caretakers will take on must match the local culture. It does no good to offer a workshop if no one attends. In that case, moderating expectations about what people will do and offering on-site training for a more limited role may be the most that can be accomplished. Every community will be different, but in general, the more populous the area, the more likely workshops will attract a steady flow of attendees.

Workshops can serve several purposes. Foremost is to teach caretakers how to safely trap all their cats and get them spayed or neutered. Mass trapping — the TNR of all the cats in a colony at once — should be the approach taught if local spay/neuter providers can accommodate entire colonies at a time. Mass trapping quickly remedies what might be an out-of-control situation, stopping reproduction

> Training people how to interact with service providers will make the process of using services smoother, encouraging providers' continued participation in the TNR program.

and calming neighbors disturbed by cats' nuisance behavior. It is also easier to catch all the cats at the same time than to go one-by-one and eventually have to pick out the last ones from the rest of the colony. There are economies of scale as well, as transportation, arranging holding space, securing equipment and all the other steps need only be done once.

Mass trapping is described in detail in the "Neighborhood Cats TNR Handbook," 2nd edition, and demonstrated in the instructional video, "How to Perform a Mass Trapping," both available at no cost at www.neighborhoodcats.org for use in educational settings.

Steps to the mass trapping process to cover in a workshop include:

- Establishing a feeding pattern
- Cataloging the cats
- Arranging a holding space
- Scheduling spay/neuter appointments
- Securing equipment
- Performing the trapping
- Caring for confined cats before and after surgery.

To enhance the learning process, workshop graduates could participate in scheduled trappings for in-field training.

Caretakers can also be taught best practices for the long-term care of the cats. Practical topics could include how to deal with neighbors, ways to keep cats out of gardens and yards, and inexpensive means for boosting nutrition and providing winter shelter.

By providing workshops, the TNR program has the opportunity to set the standards of care for how TNR will be practiced in that community. If caretakers are told not to test every cat for FIV or FeLV, this will become the norm and not a matter of controversy. Answers to questions such as how long cats should be held for recovery post-surgery, when relocation is appropriate, or what vaccinations should be routinely administered will be determined by what is taught at the workshops.

Workshops can also acquaint caretakers with the procedures of service providers. For a spay/neuter clinic, these may include paperwork to be completed ahead of time, drop-off and pickup times, the need to bring each cat in a separate, covered trap, and the cost of optional veterinary services. Training people how to interact with service providers will make the process of using services smoother, encouraging providers' continued participation in the TNR program.

One option to consider is making workshop attendance mandatory in exchange for access to other TNR services, such as discount spay/neuter surgeries, free trap rentals, food giveaways and expert assistance. This ensures everyone working with the TNR program has basic training and knows how the local system works. The program could then distribute a list of attendees to service providers or provide attendees with a certificate or card to present when arranging services.

Spay/neuter services

The availability of free or very low-cost spay/neuter surgeries is essential for TNR to be widely practiced throughout a community. Because there are usually multiple cats in a colony, the bill can mount up quickly otherwise. For an owner of a pet cat, a $50 fee for spay or neuter surgery would be considered very reasonable in most areas. But if a caretaker is feeding 10 cats, the equivalent colony sterilization fee would be $500, too high a price for most caretakers, especially those on fixed incomes who may already be struggling to pay for cat food.

In most cases, the spay/neuter provider's actual cost of a surgery is likely to exceed what caretakers can reasonably be charged without discouraging widespread participation in the TNR program. This means the program itself must subsidize the surgeries and keep the price to caretakers as low as possible. In the ideal situation, TNR programs would fully subsidize surgeries and offer services free to caretakers. This makes sense considering that caretakers, even without having to pay the veterinary costs, are still bearing other expenses, such as bait, food and transportation, and donating their time and labor. But tight program budgets often mean fully subsidized surgeries may not be feasible and some co-payment for spay/neuter surgery is needed. Many programs have successfully charged caretakers a co-pay of anywhere from $10 to $20 per cat and still been able to fill available surgery slots.

> When scheduling appointments, slots should be allocated by colony, not caretaker, in order to further colony-level targeting.

When scheduling appointments, slots should be allocated by colony, not caretaker, in order to further colony-level targeting. This can be illustrated by a hypothetical TNR program that has 20 surgeries available and appointments sought by four caretakers, each with a colony of 10 cats. It might seem fair to divide the number of surgeries by the number of caretakers and allocate five slots to each. However, this would mean all four colonies would achieve only a 50% sterilization rate, not high enough to further population reduction in any of the four. A more effective approach would be to allocate the 20 slots to two colonies and achieve a 100% sterilization rate in those two. That way, numbers would start to decline in the treated colonies. When more surgeries became available, the program could target the remaining two colonies as well.

Ways to deliver spay/neuter surgeries in a cost-effective manner range from in-house surgical suites and private veterinarian networks to high-volume spay/neuter clinics and mass spay days.

High-volume spay/neuter clinics

Clinics that specialize in spay/neuter surgeries and aim to sterilize large volumes of cats can often keep their costs per surgery much lower than an all-purpose veterinary clinic. The National Spay Neuter Response Team (NSNRT), a program of Humane Alliance (www.humanealliance.org), specializes in training agencies to set up and run high-volume clinics. For additional information on the logistics of running a high-quality, high-volume spay/neuter clinic focusing on free-roaming cats, see Feral Cat Spay/Neuter Project, "Our Clinic Model" at feralcatproject.org/ocm/ocm.aspx.

In-house surgical suites

When a nonprofit animal welfare organization — whether a shelter or other agency — operates its own spay/neuter surgical suite, it has control over all costs. By using its own veterinary staff and equipment and reducing fees close to actual costs, it can provide more affordable spay/neuter services.

Private veterinarian network

Recruiting local private veterinarians to support a TNR program can broaden the base of affordable spay/neuter surgeries. Many veterinarians are glad to assist in addressing cat overpopulation and will be able to provide some number of surgeries heavily discounted from their normal rates. In a town with an estimated population of several hundred free-roaming cats, a veterinarian who can offer five discounted surgeries a week will go a long way towards solving the problem.

Veterinarians and their staff may need some training on how best to handle feral cats, such as not transferring cats from traps into cages and using trap dividers to feed and clean. Programs should also provide information on how to perform a correct eartip, along with photos of properly tipped cats. For reference, informative articles on veterinary care for feral cats can be found in Animal Sheltering magazine and Veterinary Technician magazine.[18]

Mass spay days

An extremely cost-efficient method for delivering spay/neuter surgeries for feral cats is a large one day or weekend clinic capable of sterilizing anywhere from 100 to 200 cats per day. These clinics bring together several veterinarians and veterinary technicians, who often donate their time. Many lay volunteers perform tasks such as check-in, cleaning ears, weighing cats, monitoring post-surgical recovery and other duties. The space used is often donated as well — a large open room with an adjoining surgical suite is ideal. Because there is a fair amount of work involved in organizing these clinics and a limit to volunteers' availability, agencies which perform mass spay days typically hold them no more than once a month.

This method offers the advantage of making it much easier for veterinarians and veterinary staff to participate in a TNR program. Instead of trying to work feral cat spay/neuter surgeries into their own

---

[18] Brenda Griffin, DVM, "Returning Healthy Feral Cats — Tips for veterinary care during trap-neuter-return," Animal Sheltering January/February 2013: 53-57. (www.animalsheltering.org/resources/magazine/jan-feb-2013/returning-healthy-feral-cats.pdf).

See also, Nancy Peterson, RVT, "Caring for Feral Cats in the Clinic," Veterinary Technician August 2006: 498-505. (www.animalsheltering.org/resources/sample/cat-samples/article-caring-for-feral-cats.pdf).

private practices, they can donate services for a day a month and still make a significant contribution. Mass spay days also offer savings from economies of scale and not having to maintain a fixed facility.

Detailed protocols for administering a mass spay day are available from Operation Catnip (www.vetmed.ufl.edu/ extension-outreach/operation-catnip/), a Gainesville, Fla., agency which routinely alters 200 cats in a single day.

Trap bank procedures

As explained in the previous training section, mass trapping is the preferred method when targeting colonies. Few caretakers, however, will be willing or financially able to buy the number of traps needed, especially if they plan to trap only their colony and not pursue TNR further. Caretakers might purchase one or two traps for their own use, but not 10 or 15. The TNR program must provide the equipment if mass trapping is going to become standard practice.

Traps purchased should be from 30 to 36 inches in length and have a sliding, guillotine-type rear door. A minimum of 30 inches is needed so the trap has enough interior space to double as a cage after a cat is captured. Absent special circumstances, such as an

ill cat who needs extra care, a cat being TNR'd will be confined for no more than several days. For this short duration, the trap will adequately serve as a cage, avoiding the risks of injury and escape when cats are transferred from traps into cages. Traps also take up less room, facilitating the TNR of multiple cats at once. The sliding rear door is essential so the trap can be accessed at both ends for feeding and cleaning.

Trap dividers are also needed, so that the cat can be sectioned off on one end while the door on the other is opened for feeding and cleaning. Almost every trap manufacturer also makes a divider, but not all dividers are strong enough to be safe for these purposes. Check the "Neighborhood Cats TNR Handbook," 2nd edition, for their trap recommendations. Always use dividers in pairs, placing them back to back in the trap, for additional security. It is not necessary to buy a pair for each trap, as the same pair of dividers can be used for all cats trapped as part of the same project. Have at least a few pairs in inventory so that there will be enough dividers available if multiple projects are going on simultaneously.

Sometimes, people are initially concerned that the practice of housing cats in traps could be inhumane. In fact, traps fit well with a feral cat's nature. When confined, ferals prefer tight, dark spaces to ones that are open and bright. As long as the cats are provided food and water and the trap is kept covered with a sheet, has the floor lined with thick newspaper and is cleaned twice a day, they do just fine. If it is necessary to place a feral in a cage for any reason, it is important to also provide a feral cat den, carrier or even a cardboard box so the cat will have somewhere tight and dark to hide. Friendly cats also adjust to confinement in traps, though they tend to be more vocal than ferals.

When deciding how many traps to have on hand, a good rule of thumb is to have twice the TNR program's weekly surgical capacity. So if the TNR program plans to alter an average of 20 cats a week, it will need

40 traps. The reason for needing twice the surgical capacity is that the traps double as cages. The use of a trap as a cage begins when the cat is captured, continues through any pre-surgical holding period and ends after a minimum of 24 hours of post-surgical recovery time. This entire process can take up to several days. It will be easier to manage if the caretakers scheduled for the following week's surgeries can pick up their traps and get started without having to wait until the current TNR projects are fully completed.

It is a good idea to also have one or more drop traps in stock. A normal trap, referred to as a "box trap," works when a cat enters through the front door and then walks to the back to get the bait, stepping on a plate along the way which causes the front door to shut behind her. Cats are naturally wary of entering a box trap and food must be withheld the day before the trapping so they are hungry enough to overcome their fear. In contrast, a drop trap is propped up off the ground and a cat must walk under it to reach the bait. Once the cat is eating, the trapper pulls a string or triggers a remote control device and the trap falls down over the cat. The cat is then transferred into a box trap or transfer cage.

Most cats are not fearful of going under a drop trap and don't need to be as hungry or deprived of food for as long when compared to using box traps. A drop trap is thus an excellent tool for cats who are more difficult to capture. It is also useful for selective

trapping, such a pregnant female or the one cat in the colony who hasn't been sterilized yet. The use of drop traps does require training and some practice, but these traps are invaluable once mastered. They are now mass produced and commercially available.

Regarding trap bank procedures, programs should avoid scheduling unique pickup and drop-off times for individual caretakers. When people run late or do not appear, this can waste a lot of time for program staff. Instead, it is best to designate specific one-hour or two-hour periods during the week when the trap bank is open and let caretakers arrange to come at those times. Traps will be damaged or lost in the course of events, so take deposits. The deposit does not always have to be the full value of all traps and dividers borrowed — this might be prohibitive for someone who needs a large number — but it should be enough to ensure return of the equipment. Borrowers should also be responsible for cleaning the traps prior to returning them.

Communication essentials

A key audience a grassroots mobilization program will need to reach is members of the public who are seeking assistance with free-roaming cats and may have never heard of TNR. It is best for this audience and the TNR program when all local animal welfare organizations are sending the same message. If the system in place is to train interested members of the public at a workshop before giving attendees access to free and discount services, then anyone seeking help should be informed of this two-step process, no matter which agency they contact first. Ideally, if the volume of inquiries is not too great for one group to handle, first-time callers and email inquiries would be forwarded to the grassroots effort's lead agency for response. Having one point of contact would ensure uniformity of message. One way to facilitate this is to have a hotline publicized by all participating organizations and manned by the lead agency.

A central website can serve dual purposes. It can provide a basic introduction to TNR to those seeking help for the first time plus contact details to get more information. It can also be a resource center for those already practicing TNR by listing all relevant services available in the community and how to access them. This could include information on trap banks, workshops, spay/neuter providers, trapping assistance and advice, transportation, humane deterrents for keeping cats out of gardens and yards, and winter shelter sales or giveaways. In some communities, the lead agency's own website could serve the purpose of a central TNR website. In others a shared site administered by the lead agency in the name of the community TNR program might work best. What should be avoided is scattering important information across numerous websites of various organizations, making it difficult for anyone to easily find what they need. When administering a website, the lead agency should at all times be mindful of protecting confidential information and not using licensed materials without proper authorization.

A TNR program can stretch its resources by connecting caretakers to one another and enabling them to work together to solve logistical problems, such as arranging transport to a clinic on surgery day or finding someone to fill in and feed a colony for a few days. This can be done in different ways. An email or text message network administered by the lead agency can send out alerts to caretakers in the community with contact information for the person needing help. The San Antonio Feral Cat Coalition in San Antonio, Texas, has an extensive email list of caretakers gathered from the thousands of residents it has trained in its workshops over the past several years. When someone needs assistance, the group targets the email request to caretakers in the part of the city where the request originated. They report great success in making those connections. Online discussion groups and other social media are other ways for caretakers to network directly.

Caretaker support

Having a strong base of caretakers will greatly enhance a grassroots mobilization initiative. To help develop this base, a TNR program can provide material support in addition to connecting caretakers with one another. TNR projects can be intimidating for someone who has never trapped before. Offering a newcomer the assistance of an expert volunteer, especially on the first day of a mass trapping, can go a long way towards getting all the cats caught and altered. If an expert cannot be physically present, then being available by phone or email to give advice and guidance can also be of benefit.

Once the cats are spayed and neutered, their ongoing care becomes the primary concern. Food is the major expense. In most communities, it would be too large a burden for a TNR program to take on the responsibility of providing food for all colonies. Nonetheless, caretakers will welcome any donations. Programs can arrange food drives if there is a convenient location where people can drop off bags and cans and the food can be stored for a couple of weeks before being distributed. If not, a holiday event is another option. Invitations to the event can ask each attendee to bring a bag of cat food and caretakers can come by afterwards to take the donations away.

Shelter is also a constant need for free-roaming cats and is a particular concern during winter in colder climates when it is vital for cats to have warm, dry places to sleep. Arranging for the manufacture and delivery of shelters will save caretakers from having to build shelters themselves. TNR programs that can afford it can distribute shelters for free or at a partially subsidized cost. For groups with fewer resources, shelters can be supplied at cost. Middle to late fall is usually a good time to distribute winter shelters.

Helping find homes for young kittens and friendly adult cats is another way a TNR program can help caretakers. When colonies are first TNR'd, kittens are frequently present and individual caretakers may have few options for placing them. Taking kittens and friendlies is one way rescue groups and shelters with cage space can participate in the community program. This both supports caretakers and causes an immediate drop in the free-roaming population. If local animal welfare groups do not have space, then the TNR program can post adoptables on an online adoption site, providing wider visibility than they would likely get otherwise. If kittens need to be socialized or are very young and need bottle-feeding, the TNR program or other knowledgeable groups can provide training in these areas.

Colony registration

Every TNR program should collect data that will assist in administering and evaluating the impact of a grassroots effort. Towards this end, a colony registration system can be an important tool. At a minimum, registration data would include the location of the colony and the caretaker's identity and contact information. By having this information, a TNR program can maintain communication with caretakers, keeping them apprised of any new developments in their area, such as a rabies outbreak. Knowledge of colony locations can also help the program return eartipped cats turned into local shelters. Cats are very territorial and if the program is told where an eartipped cat was picked up, it can search its database of colonies and contact caretakers in the same vicinity.

By also recording the number of cats in each colony and how many of those cats are altered, the TNR program will have some basis for evaluating the effectiveness of its grassroots efforts. As colony sizes go down and sterilization percentages rise, the program will have increasing impact. This data can also help identify caretakers who need extra assistance, such as one with a large colony but few cats altered.

Other data points that can be informative are the number of cats and kittens from each colony placed for adoption, and the spay/neuter provider or providers used for TNR. Note that what is being tracked are colonies, not individual cats. Recording each cat and its history will greatly increase the complexity and administrative burden of a registration system. While this information may be useful for individual caretakers, it is of less value to the TNR program.

Programs can capture the registration data using basic database software, either desktop or cloud-based. If TNR program personnel will handle data entry, the information collected should be limited in order to minimize time required. If there is too much data being gathered compared to the capacity of the program to enter and track the details, the data could become stale and incomplete over time. Some TNR programs, such as the one run by Neighborhood Cats in New York City, have developed online databases that allow each caretaker to enter her own colony information, virtually eliminating data entry demands on the TNR program itself.

Who will hold and have access to the data should be decided from the outset. In some jurisdictions with a TNR-enabling ordinance, the ordinance itself requires registration with a specific agency. Absent such a mandate, in most cases the lead agency for the grassroots mobilization program will be in the best position to both collect and make use of the data. However, if the lead agency is a governmental unit or agent, there might be problems with keeping the data confidential.

Most states have freedom of information acts, also known as open records or sunshine laws. These laws give any member of the public the right to copies of government records that are not specifically exempted from disclosure. This could include colony data held by an animal control agency or other municipal unit or agent. Most caretakers want their identities and colony locations kept confidential and may not provide the information if this cannot be guaranteed. This issue can be avoided if the agency administering the colony registration system is non-governmental and exempt from public disclosure laws. In some states, it is possible for a private agency to be deemed a government unit for purposes of these laws because it is playing a governmental role. A knowledgeable attorney should be consulted whenever there is a question about the status of a particular agency or when any legal issues arise with respect to exchange of data or ownership of data collected.

If the agency holding the colony registration system can guarantee confidentiality, it should do so expressly and list any other organizations or individuals who will have access to the data and for what purposes. For example, the TNR program may intend to share non-specific data, such as the total number of colonies and cats, for statistical or research purposes. Being completely open about this will encourage caretakers to participate. Another concern is the history of the agency holding the records with respect to TNR and the treatment of community cats. If the agency had a past policy of trapping

> Who will hold and have access to the data should be decided from the outset.

and euthanizing cats, caretakers may be reluctant to reveal their identities and colony locations. In these circumstances, the TNR program will benefit from having the colony registration system administered by an organization known and trusted by caretakers.

Aligning its policies in support of TNR is another important role an animal control agency can play.

Role of animal control agencies

An animal control agency can hasten the progress of a grassroots TNR program even if it is not actively involved in the trapping and releasing of free-roaming cats. As discussed, the return of eartipped cats to their colonies after they have been turned in to an animal control shelter will both save cats' lives and build confidence among caretakers. This safety net requires the animal control agency to promptly notify the TNR program's lead agency when eartipped cats are intaked.

Aligning its policies in support of TNR is another important role an animal control agency can play. These new policies could include not sending out officers to trap cats, not picking up cats trapped by others unless the cat is injured or ill or there is a public health risk and only lending out traps for TNR purposes. This sends a clear message to the community that the correct way to handle free-roaming cats is with TNR and if residents want to take another approach, they will have to do so at their own time and expense.

Animal control can also refer callers with complaints about cats to the TNR program, making it clear there is an alternative available besides removal. Finally, because of their professional standing, animal control officers and agency officials can be among the most persuasive advocates when it comes to educating residents and property owners about TNR.

Grassroots mobilization case study

Neighborhood Cats and New York City

Over eight million people live in New York City with the number of free-roaming cats estimated to be at least in the tens of thousands. The scale of cat overpopulation is beyond the capacity of any one group or even multiple organizations to effectively address using only their own resources. In this setting, grassroots mobilization is critical to success. Since 1999, that has been the strategy pursued by Neighborhood Cats, a TNR group based in New York.

Neighborhood Cats was founded when a few neighbors on the Upper West Side of Manhattan TNR'd a colony of approximately 30 cats living in the courtyard of one square block. At that time, no organized TNR services were publicly available. The group's founders recruited local private veterinarians, secured discount rates and went about trapping the cats one by one. It took nine months to get most of the cats sterilized, but by the time the colony was under control, it was clear TNR had greatly improved the situation. Adoptions of kittens from the colony resulted in fewer cats on site. Once the nuisance behavior abated, residents of adjacent apartment buildings more readily accepted the cats' presence.

Word spread quickly about the project and other caretakers in the neighborhood wanted to TNR their colonies as well. Over the next couple of years, Neighborhood Cats volunteers assisted with trapping throughout the Upper West Side, resulting in a dramatic drop in cat intake from those ZIP codes to the city's animal control agency, now known as Animal Care & Control of New York City (ACC). Convinced TNR was a viable approach in a densely populated urban area like New York, Neighborhood Cats lobbied ACC for support. ACC adjusted its policies to favor TNR, ending the trapping of cats by animal control officers, and began notifying Neighborhood Cats when eartipped cats came into their facilities. A pilot project involved ACC's hands-on participation in the TNR of several colonies.

Requests for assistance started coming in from throughout the city and the volume grew too high for a handful of volunteers to manage. So that interested residents could learn to perform TNR themselves, Neighborhood Cats offered training workshops at venues throughout the city, including public library conference rooms and other meeting spaces. Residents from all five boroughs attended and several of the early attendees went on to form their own TNR nonprofits. Instructors emphasized colony-level targeting and sterilizing as close to all of the cats in a colony as possible.

The grassroots effort greatly accelerated when local spay/neuter clinics offered free spay/neuter surgeries for feral cats at their mobile clinics, making attendance at the Neighborhood Cats workshop a requirement to schedule appointments. The availability of free surgeries made it possible to TNR entire colonies at a time, and Neighborhood Cats developed the technique of mass trapping and taught the technique to attendees. Workshop attendance also became a prerequisite for accessing other TNR services such as trap banks, online caretaker networks and expert assistance. Neighborhood Cats created a "TNR Coach" program, paying experienced trappers a stipend to assist recent workshop attendees on their first day of mass trapping.

To track TNR activity, Neighborhood Cats developed an online database that caretakers could access remotely to enter their own information. The colony database, together with a caretaker email list compiled from workshop attendees, provided the information needed to successfully return eartipped cats turned in to ACC. The group also built a website listing all TNR services offered by the different groups in New York City.

Other actions taken to promote participation in TNR included a high profile project on Rikers Island where New York City's main jail complex was spread over 400 acres and housed more than 11,000 inmates in the largest jail facility in the country. Neighborhood Cats coordinated a joint effort by the city's major animal welfare agencies to spay or neuter approximately 300 cats in four months. The project garnered local and national media attention and boosted interest in TNR.

Neighborhood Cats realized early on that a grassroots, colony-by-colony approach in a city as large as New York would need to be sustained for many years. The organization improved its fundraising, hired full-time staff and laid the foundation for a lasting presence. To date, more than 5,000 residents have been trained at workshops. Neighborhood Cats conservatively estimates between 50,000 to 75,000 community cats have been TNR'd city-wide since the organization's founding. Impact from the grassroots TNR program is difficult to assess because of the length and size of the effort and the influence of other programs running concurrently. But one point that is clear is the 36% drop in cat intake to ACC since 2009 (Figure 31). Three factors can be identified as possible causes for this decline. The first and most obvious was the reduction in ACC services in 2010

Figure 31. **Cat intake: Animal Care & Control of New York City**

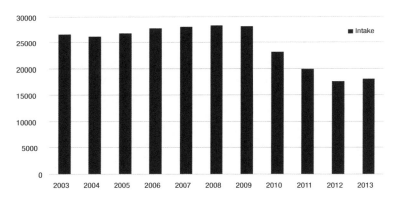

due to budget cuts. In February 2010, hours at one of ACC's primary shelter facilities were reduced from 24 to 12 a day. Later, in September 2010, cuts were made in field services and ACC's calling center, eliminating the pickup by ACC staff of cats trapped by residents. These changes in shelter policies likely account for at least some portion of the drop in cat intake in 2010 and 2011. Notably, however, intake continued to drop in 2012 and stayed down in 2013, despite budget increases and reinstatement of many of the previously slashed services. One service not reinstated was the pickup of trapped cats. ACC's current policy is to pick up only cats who are injured, ill or presenting a public health risk.

A second factor behind the drop in cat intake starting in 2010 was the work of local animal welfare organizations to spay or neuter the pets of low-income owners throughout the city. In the past decade, substantial resources have been dedicated to this effort, resulting in the altering of many thousands of pet cats.

Finally, there is the grassroots TNR program. It may have taken until 2010 before enough colonies had been targeted for population decline among community cats to start impacting intake numbers. At the end of 2013, the Neighborhood Cats colony database had registered more than 2,000 colonies that collectively totaled more than 21,000 cats. Since the time TNR had started in each colony, on average the number of cats had reportedly declined by 30%.

While the statistical impact of the grassroots mobilization program led by Neighborhood Cats cannot be determined beyond the reported average reduction in colony size, the years-long effort has led to TNR becoming the preferred approach to managing community cats in New York City. In 2012, as a sign of support, the New York City Council mandated that the city's Department of Health and Mental Hygiene post links to local TNR programs on the department's website.

Trap-Neuter-Return is no longer a movement in its infancy in the United States, but is now the driving force behind efforts to bring free-roaming cat populations under control humanely and effectively.

7.

Position Statements

Trap-Neuter-Return is no longer a movement in its infancy in the United States, but is now the driving force behind efforts to bring free-roaming cat populations under control humanely and effectively. The mainstream adoption of TNR is reflected in the position statements related to the subject by some of the leading national animal welfare organizations. These statements can be a powerful tool for advocates of new TNR programs, proving the widespread acceptance of the method. For this purpose, the position statements of Alley Cat Allies, Best Friends Animal Society, PetSmart Charities and The Humane Society of the United States are reproduced here.

Alley Cat Allies' Position on Trap-Neuter-Return

Trap-Neuter-Return (TNR) is the only humane and effective approach for outdoor cats. Scientific studies show TNR improves the lives of cats, improves their relationships with people, and reduces cat populations over time. After nearly three decades of TNR in the United States, entire colonies of cats have slowly diminished in size and are now nonexistent—zero cats in the colony—as a result.

Outdoor cats, often called feral or community cats, are the same species as pet cats, Felis catus—it is just socialization that separates them, but even that distinction is flexible. This population is a leading source of pet cats. More than a third—34%—of all cat-owning households adopted at least one cat as a stray.[19] The interconnectedness of indoor and outdoor cat populations is undeniable, and it's more accurate to treat them as one dynamic population of cats—stray, feral, pet, and everything in between. To improve the lives of cats, we must address the population as a whole, and TNR works with an understanding of this fluid population.

TNR dates back to the 1950s in the United Kingdom. After decades of gaining momentum in Europe, TNR made its way across the Atlantic in the 1980s, prompting the formation of a few local groups. As the movement grew, the need for a leader emerged. Alley Cat Allies formed in 1990, becoming the first national organization dedicated to improving the lives of all cats. By creating a national network of TNR advocates, distributing sought-

---

[19] Chu K, Anderson WM, Rieser MY. Population Characteristics and Neuter Status of Cats Living in Households in the United States. J Am Vet Med Assoc 2009; 234:1023-1030.

after materials, acquiring national news coverage, and advocating for cats both owned and unowned, Alley Cat Allies galvanized the TNR movement in the United States.

In a TNR program, cats are humanely trapped and brought to a veterinarian to be spayed/neutered, vaccinated, and eartipped—the tip of the left ear is removed while the cat is anesthetized to identify the cat as neutered and vaccinated. After a short recovery period they are returned to their outdoor homes.

Alley Cat Allies supports the best practice of vaccinating all cats, including rabies vaccinations, which is the protocol for Trap-Neuter-Return (sometimes called Trap-Neuter-Vaccinate-Return). Ron Cash oversees the Atlantic City, N.J., Department of Health and Human Services and is confident that "TNR is good public health policy." Cash has seen TNR benefit the Atlantic City Boardwalk's cat population and says, "they're coexisting with people very well now." A TNR program has been in place since 2001 for the colonies of cats under the famous Atlantic City, N.J., boardwalk.

A Shift in the Treatment of Cats

Today, TNR is successfully practiced in hundreds of communities across the country, in every landscape and setting. There has been a sea change in the treatment of cats in the U.S.

Some communities seek to address feral cat populations through TNR legislation, and while these efforts often mean well, it is important that they don't create barriers. Mandatory registration of cats and caregivers should never be part of TNR ordinances, and in general, ordinances should promote sterilization and vaccination and support cat caregivers. More than 430 local governments now endorse TNR, and that number is growing.

TNR stabilizes and decreases populations humanely, improves and protects cats' lives, saves taxpayer dollars, and answers community needs. Most important, TNR works—other methods do not. Investing in TNR demonstrates a socially responsible, compassionate, and efficient approach to serving animals and the public.

Cats Live Healthy Lives Outdoors

The outdoors is a feral or community cat's natural home. For more than 10,000 years, cats have lived outdoors in and around human settlements. Until the invention of litter in the 1950s, very few cats lived indoors full time. Cats continue to live healthy lives outside. Studies show outdoor cats have equally low disease rates as pet cats.

Alley Cat Allies supports best practices established by expert veterinarians, including not routinely testing for FeLV or FIV. As veterinarians explain, a test result is not a diagnosis. While some TNR programs do include routine testing, Alley Cat Allies instead supports allocating resources to increase spay and neuter.

Conflicts Can Be Resolved Humanely

A key element of TNR is establishing friendly dialogue with residents and addressing any concerns. Public workshops, door-to-door visits, and explanatory flyers are the first steps of helping stakeholders understand why TNR is the only option. Community members receive educational materials on how to live with outdoor cats and on humane deterrents and repellents, some of which are no-cost and others at various price levels.

Conflicts can usually be resolved, and removing cats from an area is almost never a valid option. When cats are removed, new cats move in or those left behind breed to capacity. This natural and scientifically documented phenomenon is called the "vacuum effect." Catching and killing cats is not only cruel, but ineffective. Other methods of removing cats, like adoption, sanctuaries, and relocation, are rarely the right choice.

While TNR programs typically include adoption for socialized cats and kittens, it is unrealistic to expect to adopt feral cats into homes. Some feral cats might make a slow, steady transition to living indoors, but most will not make that transition. "Socializing" feral cats is time-consuming and has a very low success rate.

Similarly, sanctuaries, though usually well-meaning, do nothing to stabilize the cat population. There will never be enough sanctuaries to house every cat. What's more, feral cats who are used to living outdoors suffer from stress and disease in these facilities.

Relocation is also ineffective, as it causes the vacuum effect. It also endangers cats' lives and causes them stress and suffering. Instead of uprooting cats from their home, the focus should be education and community relations.

New Approach Benefits All Cats—Not Just Feral Cats

Rounding up and removing cats—as has been done for decades—ends up killing millions of feral cats and pet cats every year. Research shows that owned cats have a better chance of finding their way home outdoors than they do in a shelter. Only 2% of cats in shelters are reclaimed by their owner.

Many shelter and animal control experts recommend including all outdoor cats in TNR programs, and suggest that shelters not accept any cat—feral, stray, or pet—who will not be adopted, contending that they have better outcomes outdoors.

Including all outdoor cats in a TNR program saves them from being killed in a shelter, and allows shelters to focus adoption and fostering efforts on cats who will have positive outcomes. Instituting a shelter-based TNR program has been shown to increase adoption rates and decrease "euthanasia" rates—changes that serve the whole cat population.

A Need for More Change

Alley Cat Allies believes our nation's shelter system needs a complete transformation. The number one documented cause of death for cats in the U.S. is being killed in shelters. More than 70% of cats entering shelters are killed—including nearly 100% of feral cats, who cannot be adopted. For decades, animal control policy has wasted millions of dollars catching and "euthanizing" healthy outdoor cats, but has failed to stabilize cat populations. With a successful program like TNR to turn to, no feral cat should be impounded. Alley Cat Allies believes it is unacceptable for animal control agencies and shelters to continue killing cats. TNR is one part of a comprehensive line of best practices that shelters should follow, including neutering before adoption and early-age spay/neuter of kittens. It is time to put an end to ineffective policies that cause more cats to be killed.

More than 80% of Americans believe it is more humane to leave a cat outside than to have her caught and killed, according to a 2007 study conducted by Harris Interactive for Alley Cat Allies. TNR reflects Americans' humane ethic that cats deserve to live out their lives in their outdoor homes.

Best
Friends
Animal
Society

Trap Neuter Return
Best Friends Animal Society Position

Best Friends Animal Society endorses and practices Trap/Neuter/Return (TNR) as the most efficient, humane and effective method for managing community cat populations. While euthanizing a suffering animal is an act of mercy, killing healthy unowned, free-roaming cats is, just like killing healthy owned cats, unacceptable and demonstrates a lack of respect for their most basic interests. TNR has been shown to stabilize and reduce colony size over time. [1-7]

Background

Historically, there have been very few positive outcomes for stray, abandoned, and feral cats (also known as "community cats") entering shelters. Today, shelters are under increasing pressure from policymakers and the public eager to make their community "no-kill," and are therefore embracing TNR as a humane and effective alternative to lethal methods.

Best Friends supports TNR as the only method for managing community cat populations because no other method has been shown to be humane and effective. In addition, a comprehensive TNR program can save local governments money. [8, 9]

References

1. Levy, J.K., D.W. Gale, and L.A. Gale, Evaluation of the effect of a long-term trap-neuter-return and adoption program on a free-roaming cat population. Journal of the American Veterinary Medical Association, 2003. 222(1): p. 42–46. http://avmajournals.avma.org/doi/abs/10.2460/javma.2003.222.42

2. Stoskopf, M.K. and F.B. Nutter, Analyzing approaches to feral cat management—one size does not fit all. Journal of the American Veterinary Medical Association, 2004. 225(9): p. 1361–1364. www.ncbi.nlm.nih.gov/pubmed/15552309 http://avmajournals.avma.org/toc/javma/225/9

3. Nutter, F.B., Evaluation of a Trap-Neuter-Return Management Program for Feral Cat Colonies: Population Dynamics, Home Ranges, and Potentially Zoonotic Diseases, in Comparative Biomedical Department 2005, North Carolina State University: Raleigh, NC. p. 224.

4. Natoli, E., et al., Management of feral domestic cats in the urban environment of Rome (Italy). Preventive Veterinary Medicine, 2006. 77(3-4): p. 180–185. www.sciencedirect.com/science/article/B6TBK-4M33VSW-1/2/0abfc80f245 ab50e602f93060f88e6f9 www.kiccc.org.au/pics/FeralCatsRome2006.pdf

5. Mendes-de-Almeida, F., et al., The Impact of Hysterectomy in an Urban Colony of Domestic Cats (Felis catus Linnaeus, 1758). International Journal of Applied Research in Veterinary Medicine, 2006. 4(2): p. 134–141. www.jarvm.com/articles/Vol4Iss2/Mendes.pdf

6. Mendes-de-Almeida, F., et al., Reduction of feral cat (Felis catus Linnaeus 1758) colony size following hysterectomy of adult female cats. Journal of Feline Medicine & Surgery, 2011

7. Robertson, S.A., A review of feral cat control. Journal of Feline Medicine & Surgery, 2008. 10(4): p. 366–375.

8. Hamilton, F.E., Leading and Organizing Social Change for Companion Animals. Anthrozoös, 2010. 23(3): p. 277–292. www.ingentaconnect. com/content/berg/anthroz/2010/00000023/00000003/art00006

9. Zawistowski, S., Simulating different approaches for managing free-roaming cat populations, in 2013 National Council on Pet Population Research Symposium Presentations: CATS: The Ins and Outs: Improving their Future Through Research 2013, Society of Animal Welfare Administrators Tempe, AZ.

PetSmart Charities TNR Position

PetSmart Charities is the leading funder of animal welfare in North America — supporting community efforts in all 50 states and Canada. The largest portion of our funding is for spay/neuter, including free-roaming cats. We are also innovators of new programs designed to stem the overpopulation of cats and reduce the euthanasia of millions of cats a year in our shelters.

As a leader in pet adoptions, helping to find homes for over 400,000 cats and dogs a year, PetSmart Charities is acutely aware of the cat overpopulation crisis in North America. Unaltered, free-roaming cats represent the largest source of homeless cats today. Left unaddressed, they result in more kittens and cats than shelters can adequately house, leading to overcrowding and euthanasia. Public health, wildlife conservation and the cats' own welfare can also be negatively impacted when free-roaming cats are left to multiply unchecked.

Trap-Neuter-Return (TNR) is currently the most humane and effective method known for reducing and managing free-roaming cat populations. TNR involves trapping, spaying or neutering, vaccinating and marking for identification healthy, unadoptable cats who are then returned to their original locations. Adequate food and shelter is either provided or available. Once altered, the cats no longer reproduce, causing their numbers to decline over time, and their nuisance behavior abates, making them better neighbors.

At PetSmart Charities, we have funded and collaborated on numerous TNR projects which have dramatically lowered intake, euthanasia and the cats' numbers. Freed from the flood of kittens and cats, shelters are able to improve conditions in their facilities, benefiting all the animals in their care. Altered and vaccinated cats reduce public health risks while fewer cats in the environment mean less predation on wildlife.

No other approach has achieved similar results, including attempts to remove cats from the environment, usually to be euthanized. To succeed in the goal of bringing free-roaming cat overpopulation under control, the focus must be on practical, proven methods. Implemented properly, TNR works and has our full support.

THE **HUMANE** SOCIETY
OF THE UNITED STATES

The Humane Society of the United States — Position on Cats

Cats are the most popular companion animal in the U.S., with more than 86 million of them living in nearly 39 million American households.

Tens of millions more unowned cats live outdoors and usually rely on people to provide them with food and shelter.

Their sociability ranges from truly unsocialized feral cats to friendly strays cats who have become lost or have been abandoned.

The Humane Society of the United States believes that every cat deserves a life free from hunger or thirst, fear and distress, discomfort, pain, injury, or disease, and that cats at risk for these are our responsibility to care for. Regardless of whether they are owned or not, cats who are outdoors are the leading cause of cat overpopulation in communities and can be a conservation threat to at least some species of wildlife on a case-by-case basis.

Owned Cats

The decisions people make for their cats are important for their cats' health and welfare; they also play a role in cat overpopulation as a whole. We urge all cat owners to take the following steps:

Have your cats spayed or neutered. Cats can begin reproducing as early as five months of age, so they should be sterilized by that age or younger whenever possible. Cats can have more than one litter each year, and each litter adds to the millions of cats across the country competing for homes. Close to two million cats are euthanized each year in shelters and animal control facilities nationwide. In addition to population control, sterilization can also eliminate unpleasant behaviors of intact cats, such as male cats fighting and female cats going into their reproductive season.

Keep your cats safe indoors. Indoor cats live longer, tend to be healthier, and can avoid some of the predators, injuries, parasites, and communicable diseases to which outdoor cats may be exposed. Indoor cats do not kill birds and other wildlife. An outdoor enclosure or walk on a harness and leash can provide a cat with safe outdoor access, if desired, although cats do not require outdoor access to live full and happy lives.

Put visible identification on your cats at all times. Accidental escape is a common risk for indoor cats. Only about 2 percent of lost cats who enter animal shelters are claimed by their families. A collar with visible identification attached is the best life insurance you can buy. Cats can easily and safely wear collars with identification, and a microchip is a good backup means of identification. Microchips alone are not enough, since it's the visible ID that will immediately alert people that the cat is owned.

Provide regular veterinary care. All cats, even cats who
   never interact with other animals or venture outdoors,
   should be examined at least once a year and receive
   vaccinations against rabies and other diseases,
   as recommended by their veterinarian. Regular
   veterinary visits, as well as preventative care, such as
   keeping cats indoors and providing good nutrition,
   are key to ensuring the highest quality of life for cats.

Unowned Cats

The most pressing cat issue in the U.S. is the large
population of unsterilized outdoor cats. This results
in many cats without permanent/conventional homes
living in outdoor populations, quickly producing ongoing
generations of cats. These cats may be feral, meaning
they do not willingly interact with humans, while some
are semi- or formerly-owned, or otherwise friendly
cats who have been lost or abandoned. Until the day
when the population has been reduced and all cats
live in loving homes, The HSUS supports and promotes
humane management of outdoor cat populations.

To this end, we support Trap-Neuter-Return (TNR)
and similar sterilization programs, legislation that
allows for and supports non-lethal population
control, and coalition-based approaches that involve
community leaders, citizens, and stakeholders to
implement effective community cat management
programs. Programs that attempt to use lethal
control to eliminate cat populations are inhumane,
ineffective, and wasteful of scarce resources.

In standard TNR practice, cats are humanely trapped
and, if healthy, spay/neutered, rabies vaccinated,
eartipped (for identification), and returned to their
community. These programs have shown evidence of
stabilizing cat numbers that eventually dwindle to zero
as the cats naturally pass away. The HSUS believes
that the humane reduction and eventual elimination of
unowned cat populations should be the end goal for

all TNR participants and supporters. TNR should be considered a humane means to an end, not a method of permanently maintaining outdoor cat populations.

Cats in Shelters

In many areas of the U.S., unlimited admission of cats is not a legal mandate for shelters, yet millions of community (unowned and outdoor) cats are regularly admitted and, despite strong efforts by shelters, most cats do not make it out alive. Even though large numbers of cats are euthanized in shelters, the numbers do not come close to reaching a tipping point to decrease outdoor cat populations. This results in a cycle of intake and euthanasia for a small percentage of the overall cat population in a given community, with little to no impact on total numbers.

Managing cat populations in this way is not working. Instead, we as a society need to focus on finding and deploying solutions that will work — ones that will serve the interests of cats, wildlife, and communities. Shelters may consider reducing intake of healthy cats they cannot place into loving homes and can effectively use those freed-up funds to address cat overpopulation; whether that be through accessible spay/neuter programs; behavioral resources for people struggling with their owned cats; assistance with pet food, vaccines, and other services; or TNR and other non-lethal population control strategies.

Cats and Wildlife

Predation by outdoor cats on birds and other wildlife is a real and legitimate concern. While The HSUS believes that outdoor cats are entitled to protection, it also believes that wildlife populations need to be protected from cats. That's one of the reasons we actively promote TNR, and why we have been involved in programs such as the removal of feral cats from San Nicholas Island, Calif., in an effort to balance the needs of all animals, and not promote one species at the expense of others. The HSUS does not support managed colonies in ecologically sensitive areas or in areas where the cats are at imminent risk of harm, such as demolition sites or areas where nuisance complaints have escalated and remain unresolved.

The HSUS supports collaborative efforts, such as coalition-based initiatives, to humanely reduce outdoor cat populations while protecting threatened and endangered wildlife populations. The scope of the problem is so large, both geographically and in terms of the sheer number of cats, that a triage approach is needed to protect the most vulnerable wildlife populations, such as endangered species on islands. Also, incremental progress must be made to address harm done to all species of wild animals vulnerable to cat predation, as they all hold inherent value. Through wildlife-sensitive-area mapping, cat-colony relocation or feeding modification, the establishment of appropriate sanctuaries, and other innovative solutions, the negative impacts can be lessened and eventually eliminated.

Collaboration/Humane Communities

Each community is different, and there is no effective one-size-fits-all response to managing community (unowned) cats. Stakeholders must work together to create programs that address specific needs and maximize available resources in their community.

Communities will succeed when they pursue a combination of the following:

- Truly accessible spay/neuter and TNR services for pet and community cats

- Support and implementation of best practices for managing community cat colonies

- Pet food pantries, behavior assistance, and other programs to help people keep their cats in their homes

- Shelter and rescue innovations and partnerships to increase cat adoptions
- Shelter policy changes to reduce the intake of healthy community cats when euthanasia is the likely outcome
- Public education and outreach
- Adequate, enforceable cat-related ordinances and state laws

Of course, successful community programs will rely on sufficient government funding as well as private/public partnerships and significant volunteerism to support these broadly beneficial programs.

Conclusion

While the task ahead of us is complex, it is not impossible. Great efforts are already underway in a variety of cities, towns, and islands across our country and the globe. America's favorite pet deserves to live a long, healthy, and humane life, and The HSUS is dedicated to making that a reality.

A House is not a Home without paws

8.

Resources

Books

"The Neighborhood Cats TNR Handbook,"
2nd edition (Neighborhood Cats, 2013).
www.neighborhoodcats.org
(available for free download.)
An A to Z guide to the hands-on work of
Trap-Neuter-Return.

"Management of Stray and Feral Community Cats,"
by Julie K. Levy and Christine L. Wilford, Chapter 41 in
"Shelter Medicine for Veterinarians and Staff," 2nd ed,
(Wiley-Blackwell Publishers, 2013).
www.wiley.com/WileyCDA/WileyTitle/
productCd-EHEP002626.html

Community cat organizations

"Map of Feral Cat Groups in the U.S. and Canada,"
by The Humane Society of the United States
www.humanesociety.org/assets/maps/feral-cats.html
An interactive map listing groups working with
community cats in the U.S. and Canada.

Funding

PetSmart Charities
www.petsmartcharities.org/pro
Grants for TNR projects, community pets
spay/neuter and spay/neuter equipment.

Spay/neuter resources

"Spay/Neuter Clinic Locator"
www.petsmartcharities.org/spay-neuter/locator/
Enter a ZIP code and locate low-cost
spay/neuter clinics in that area.

Toolkits

"Action Kit: Advocating for TNR in Your Community,"
by Best Friends Animal Society
www.bestfriends.org/Resources
(search for the title of the Action Kit)

Contains resources to help implement
a community TNR program.

"Pets for Life Community Outreach Toolkit,"
from The Humane Society of the United States and
PetSmart Charities
www.animalsheltering.org
(search for the title of the Toolkit)

A guide to developing and implementing a
community outreach program to promote
spay/neuter in underserved areas.

Videos

"How to Perform a Mass Trapping,"
by Neighborhood Cats
www.neighborhoodcats.org

An instructional video demonstrating all steps
in a mass trapping project (32 mins.).

"Trap-Neuter-Return: Fixing Feral Cat Overpopulation,"
by The Humane Society of the United States
www.humanesociety.org/feralcats
(scroll down to bottom of page to view video)

Webinars

"Supporting Community Cats,"
by PetSmart Charities and
The Humane Society of the United States
www.petsmartcharities.org/pro
(click on "Learn," then on "Join Our
Learning Community")

A 27-part webinar series on all aspects of
Trap-Neuter-Return, consisting of three tracks:
Colony Level, Community Level and Hot Topics.

Websites

Find more information on Trap-Neuter-Return
and free-roaming cats:

Alley Cat Allies
www.alleycat.org

Best Friends Animal Society
www.bestfriends.org

Neighborhood Cats
www.neighborhoodcats.org

PetSmart Charities
www.petsmartcharities.org/pro/learn

The Humane Society of the United States
www.humanesociety.org

Acknowledgments

Like all we do on behalf of homeless pets at PetSmart Charities, this guide has been a team effort. My deepest thanks to all those listed here whose hard work, professionalism and dedication have made this publication the best it can be.

Special thanks to the animal welfare organizations and government agencies from across the country who generously shared their TNR experiences and information, and to all the community cat caretakers and volunteers who contribute to the success of TNR efforts.

Edited by Gwenn Wells.

Designed and illustrated by Chellie Buzzeo and Niel Venter. Figures and diagrams created for PetSmart Charities.

Photos by Sherrie Buzby, Neighborhood Cats, and PetSmart Charities.

Produced by PetSmart Charities Senior Communications Manager Laura Ingalls, with the assistance of Senior Director of Programs, Grants and Field Initiatives Julie White, Senior Director of Marketing, Communications and Fundraising Lisa Yoder, and Executive Director Jan Wilkins.

Thanks as well to Senior Paralegal Todd Michel for his valuable contributions.

139

22

About Bryan Kortis

Bryan Kortis currently serves as program manager for PetSmart Charities, overseeing their free-roaming cat spay/neuter grants as well as other community cat initiatives. He is the co-founder and former executive director of Neighborhood Cats. Kortis has authored and produced many of the leading educational materials on Trap-Neuter-Return (TNR), including "The Neighborhood Cats TNR Handbook," "Implementing a Community TNR Program," and the instructional video, "How to Perform a Mass Trapping." He served as a consultant to The Humane Society of the United States on their feral cat program, is a frequent presenter on free-roaming cat issues and has helped launch successful TNR programs in New York City and other communities throughout the United States. Kortis received a Bachelor of Arts degree from Cornell University and a J.D. from University of California, Berkeley.

About PetSmart Charities

PetSmart Charities is a nonprofit animal welfare organization that saves the lives of homeless pets. More than 400,000 dogs and cats find homes each year through our adoption program in all PetSmart® stores and our sponsored adoption events. PetSmart Charities grants more money to directly help pets in need than any other animal welfare group in North America, with a focus on funding spay/neuter services that help communities solve pet overpopulation. PetSmart Charities, Inc. is a 501(c)(3) organization, separate from PetSmart, Inc.

PetSmart Charities is also the leading funder of Trap-Neuter-Return (TNR) initiatives in the United States. Since 2009, the organization has awarded grants to hundreds of animal welfare organizations and municipal agencies performing intensive TNR in targeted high-need areas of their communities. In partnership with Best Friends Animal Society, PetSmart Charities has pioneered a new model of sheltering for cats, combining Return to Field with targeted TNR and achieving dramatic reductions in intake and euthanasia in pilot cities. Building on its experience, PetSmart Charities has produced a host of educational resources on TNR, including written materials, webinars, video and live presentations.